George Wyld

Christo-Theosophy

Spiritual Dynamics and the Divine and Miraculous Man

George Wyld

Christo-Theosophy
Spiritual Dynamics and the Divine and Miraculous Man

ISBN/EAN: 9783337026875

Printed in Europe, USA, Canada, Australia, Japan

Cover: Foto ©Lupo / pixelio.de

More available books at **www.hansebooks.com**

CHRISTO-THEOSOPHY,

OR SPIRITUAL DYNAMICS

AND THE DIVINE AND MIRACULOUS MAN.

BY

GEORGE WYLD, M.D., Edin.,

AUTHOR OF "THE LIFE OF JESUS CHRIST AS A CONTINUOUS NARRATIVE OF THE FOUR GOSPELS."

SECOND EDITION.

LONDON:
KEGAN, PAUL, TRENCH, TRÜBNER & Co., Limited.
1895.

Price 3/6 net.

In sending this issue forth in my 86th year, I wish most emphatically to call the special attention of my readers to the footnote on page 49, which reads thus :—

I permit this theory to stand as just written, but I now add that since writing this paper I have come much more round to the theory that most of the mediumistic phenomena of the above kind are produced by foreign spirits.

For I am as convinced now as when I wrote it of the great importance and truth of its teaching, nor during these intervening years have I swerved from my conviction.

GEORGE WYLD, M.D.

27th March, 1906.

PREFACE.

As this book has been out of print for some years, a second edition, with corrections and additions, seems to be called for; and especially because the term Theosophy is in the air, and because I feel that the reading public should know that there is and always has been a *Christian Theosophy*, which must be in antagonism to that system of Hindoo Cosmogany and Magic, vamped together by the late Madame Blavatsky.

The first edition of this book was published in 1880, when I was President of "The British Branch of the Theosophical Society," from which position I at once retired, when the foundress, in her journal, *The Theosophist* (May, 1882, Supplement, p. 6), used these words: "There is no God, personal or impersonal," for I replied, if there be no God there can be no Theosophy.

The only foundation of Theosophy, is laid in the idea—*Spirit is the Sub-stance of Matter;* and in illustration of this idea the reader is referred to the papers herein published.

The subject is one of absorbing interest, but not the less are the simple but all comprehending words of *The Master*, that in love to God and love to Man, as containing the whole of the law and the prophets, are found the whole of morality and religion, an all sufficient wisdom for the innumerable multitudes living on this earth.

WIMBLEDON,
January, 1894.

CONTENTS.

	PAGE.
I.—THE SYNOPSIS...	1
II.—THE KEY TO THEOSOPHY	3
III.—SPIRITUAL DYNAMICS...	19
IV.—MAN AS A SPIRIT	43
V.—THE DIVINE AND MIRACULOUS MAN	63
VI.—THE LIFE OF JESUS CHRIST AS AN AUTOBIOGRAPHY...	90
VII.—MIRACLES AS NOT CONTRARY TO NATURE...	101
VIII.—THE CHRISTIAN SAINTS	128
IX.—MESMERISM, HYPNOTISM, AND FAITH HEALING	150
X.—CLAIRVOYANCE AND ITS REVELATION OF THE AUTONOETIC SOUL	166
XI.—ANÆSTHETICS AND THEIR REVELATION OF THE SOUL ...	203
XII.—MATTER: AND ITS SPIRITUAL SUBSTANCES—A DEMONSTRATION	214
XIII.—BUDDHISM AND CHRISTIANITY CONTRASTED	227
XIV.—DARWINISM AND EVOLUTION	247
XV.—REINCARNATION	258
XVI.—SLEEP AND TRANCE ...	262

I.—THE SYNOPSIS.

THE highest Religion, Philosophy, Science, Poetry, and Art, are one, namely, the Still Small Voice of God speaking in the spiritual centre of the soul of man.

For as there is one God—The infinite and eternal Mind which is the substance of matter—who manifests Himself as Spirit, Force, and Phenomena, so man as the Microcosm made in the image of God, is a triune being of Spirit, Soul, and Body.

To love this one God in *Spirit* is the whole of religion, and to love thy brother and thy sister as thyself is the whole of morality.

"Therefore, hear, O Israel, the Lord thy God is one God, and thou shalt love the Lord thy God with all thy heart, and strength (and body), and soul, and mind, and thy neighbour as thyself. On these two hang all the law and the prophets, and no other commandments are greater than these."

"And where two or three are gathered together in My name, there am I in the midst."

"And behold, the kingdom of heaven is *within* you, but except ye be born of the *Spirit* ye cannot enter into that kingdom. But to him who overcometh will I give to eat of the *hidden* manna, and of the tree which is in the midst of the paradise of God."

"And to such as believe, all things are possible; and greater works shall ye do than I do; for if ye have faith as a grain of mustard seed, ye shall say to this mountain, be removed hence to yonder place, and it shall remove; and nothing shall be impossible unto you; and lo, I am with you always to the end of the world."

II.—THE KEY TO THEOSOPHY.

THEOLOGIANS dogmatically assert the existence of the soul. Many scientists make the counter assertion that there is no proof of the existence of the soul. Theosophists maintain that the existence of the soul can be demonstrated by experimental Psychology.

Theosophy signifies the knowledge, or the science, of the wisdom and will of God, and His relation to the external universe and to man.

God is the supreme unity. He is the centre and the circumference, and is thus the key to man and Christ, to earth and heaven, and to universal law. He is absolute *unity*, and thus absolute perfection; but He may be said to manifest himself as a *trinity* of Spirit, Power, and Matter.

Man as the microcosm, "is made in the image of God," and is thus also a triune being of body, soul, and spirit.

This triune nature of man as the Son, is thus the key to the nature of God as the Father, and is thus the key to Theosophy. Without this key it is impossible to know what man is, and impossible to know what Christ is, and impossible to understand scientifically how man can see God in Christ, and thus save his soul.

When, therefore, the ancients wrote on their temples, *Man, know thyself,* they enigmatically gave the key to all knowledge and all Theosophy. Because to know thyself in the centre—that is, to be born of the Spirit—is to know God.

This is the doctrine taught by the esoteric Brahmans and Buddhists, by the Kabbalistic Jews, by Pythagoras, by the Platonists, the Neo-Platonists, by Christ Himself, by St. John in the Logos, by St. Paul, by Paracelsus, by the Rosicrucians, by the Alchemists, by Jacob Bœhmen, and by the ecstatic Saints who, becoming one with Christ, thus saw and knew God.

We know our bodies to be organic machines, furnished with the five senses of hearing, seeing, smelling, tasting, and feeling, and these organs bring us *en rapport* with the external universe.

Matter, or the external universe, is the equilibrium of the forces of attraction and repulsion.

All forces are modes of action of *one* force.

Electricity has been described to me by an ecstatic in trance as the arm of God, and is thus probably, in its *essence,* the *one* force used by the Divine mind.

Thus the foundation or substance of matter is force, and the substance of force is the will of God, and the visible universe is thus only the materialised thoughts of the Divine mind.

All force manifests itself in vibrations; and all external things being the result of force, the mystery of how mind recognises external matter is explained, for as matter is only an external form of force, it is recognised by mind, which is the central force.*

The Soul is the aggregation of the mental forces, including the will, and by this soul man rules his actions and knows the external world.

The Spirit is the third factor in the triune man. It is that which is an atom or spark of the Spirit of God. It is *latent* in the natural man. It is the hidden centre or "light of every soul born into the world, and hidden from the foundation of the world." It is the secret Logos which became effulgent in the Christ, and it is that by which only God can be known. It is above and beyond reason. It is of the nature of the knowledge and wisdom and essence of God.

Thus the soul reasons on the evidences furnished by our organisation, but the spirit knows by intuition.

The soul works by physical agents, and its power is limited by mechanism. The spirit works by will, and its powers are supreme over physical law. The soul accumulates and remembers facts ; the spirit sees and knows all things.

The soul rules the body ; the spirit rules the soul, and God rules the spirit. Thus the soul is the ego of

---

* On the Nature of Perception. By R. S. Wyld, LL.D.

the body, the spirit is the ego of the soul, and God is the ego of the spirit.

As the soul is the ruler of the body in this physical world, so the spirit is the ruler of the soul in the spiritual world. The spirit is the *unity* in man, and thus is *en rapport* with the *unity* of God.

As the spirit is a unity it is indivisible, and therefore indestructible, and hence immortal.

It is by the power of the ONE that all compounds are made, and hence when man becomes a spirit, his five senses become one all-seeing and knowing sense, and as such can, like God, create forms external to himself, and thus in the world of spirits, "surround himself with the forms of his affections."

Bishop Berkeley says, "As we can only know external nature through the mind, we have no proof that nature exists externally to the mind."

This dogma the common sense of mankind rejects, and yet, in a sense, it is philosophically true, but, in the world of spirit, it is simply true, for there external forms are created by the mind, and are materialised objective thoughts.

The Heavenly habitations are described as solid and splendid mansions, and so indeed they are—solid in relation to *spirit* force, as much so as hills and trees and houses are solid in relation to the grosser quality of *soul* force.

"The Kingdom of Heaven being within us," signifies a condition of the soul and spirit, and not a position in space ; and hence, the Kingdom of Heaven may be and often is on this earth, and the departed souls of our beloved ones may, as spirits, be in our very midst.

But as " God is of purer eyes than to behold iniquity," so pure spirits, if we are sensual, may be incapable of seeing us, for our vitiating essence cannot harmonise with the subtle essence.

As men and women on this earth congregate in congenial societies, whether their nature be frivolous, vicious, selfish, or thoughtful, or holy, so in the spirit world we shall be in societies, in relation to our affections for good or evil.

Those who, while on this earth, give themselves to " the world, the flesh, and the devil," are fed by these ; but those who give themselves to truth and love and God, are ministered unto by angels.

Spiritualism, by the phenomena which come through mediums, demonstrates that there is a force connected with human beings unrecognised by what is called Science.

It claims to demonstrate the existence of the soul after death, by producing messages and visible forms, asserting that they are those of our departed friends.

Regarding the question of *identity*, I speak in another place, but here I would say that just as a Professor Owen, from the discovery of a single fossil-bone of an unknown animal could postulate the entire animal, so the philosopher from a single spiritual fact, be it only a single instance of clairvoyance, or only the moving of a chair in obedience to volition, say one yard, can construct an entire spiritual science.

The Theosophist therefore does not so much interest himself in the insatiable accumulation of spiritual phenomena as in that philosophy of spirit which is built on spiritual facts, his absorbing interest being in the nature, capabilities, and development of his own personal soul and spirit, in their relation to himself, to external nature, and to God.

The Spiritual Adept or Saint is one who has devoted himself to God, and who by a long and severe training in self-denial, commands, by means of spirit force, his own soul and nature, and thus acts as if he were a true Son of God on earth.

In relation to self-denial marriage signifies the union of the positive soul with the pure, beautiful, and intuitional spirit.

When, then, men and women unite as one in this perfect accord, marriage is the happiest of all earthly conditions, and is, moreover, not only consistent with the perfect earthly life, but essential to that life. Moreover, when two souls vibrate in perfect harmony, the result may be a Son of God.

Nevertheless and notwithstanding this, it is not the less true that the highest spiritual gifts and powers have, in all ages of the world and of the Church, been recognised as the special inheritance of the virgin and celibate.

So also Magnetic and Psychic and Pneumic healers know that their power over disease is in direct relationship to their continence, for in the Kingdom of Heaven there is neither marriage nor giving in marriage.

This is a mystery in connection with the creation of immortal souls, and with the creative force of self-denial, and hence irregularity in the sexual instinct is truly termed *dissipation*, that is, it dissipates or scatters the soul force, and is thus directly antagonistic to that soul force which, as unity, is remembrance, and by which man so controls his body as to rise to true manhood, or to that *concentration* by which true spiritual powers are obtained. Hence, all such dissipation is directly opposed to the obtaining of the spiritual or saintly power of miraculous works.

Marriage, I have said, signifies that union of soul and spirit which constitutes the perfect *Duad*. But if it ends in the physical union of man and woman, then woman as a form is worshipped in the place of spirit, the essential, and this leads to the idolatry of matter.

Thus the animal love towards the woman is the substitution of external for internal delights, and calls forth the jealousy of that "Divine Sophia," with whom those who, with profound reverence, worship God as a spirit, and thus evoke their spiritual centre and find the Logos, are united. These know that there is a spiritual marriage incompatible with that of the flesh, but regarding these matters there is also a fanaticism. And yet the females of the Mammalia have a rule in this which is of important signification, and cannot, I conceive, have arisen from physical inheritance.

Returning to adeptship, let us consider wherein lies the distinction between the adept and the spirit medium.

A spirit medium is one whose soul is easily detached from the body, and generally because that body is in a state of weakness.

This detached soul of the medium entering the world of spirit, sees and associates with other departed souls, and by their help moves tables and writes in closed spaces, or reads the mind of those present, or associates with other spirits, or as the *double*, not only acts at a distance from the body but manifests itself as a visible body, or ghost, or double, at a distance.

The soul of the medium being thus absent from the body, that body may become occupied by a wandering or foreign soul, who makes use of that body for its own ends, and may degrade or render its victims insane.

It will be seen that thus the body of the medium in trance is in a negative position, a mere body in the possession of strangers, and hence professional mediums who give promiscuous *séances*, becoming possessed by spirits of a nature analogous to the surrounding company, may on certain occasions act wisely, but too often foolishly, ignorantly, or falsely.

Even those mediums who are confined to the family circle can scarcely rise above the quality of that circle, and hence although pure and noble messages are from time to time given through such mediums, yet even these mediums, becoming surrounded by spirits in their own likeness, are apt to reflect ideas and sentiments consistent with their own desires ; and hence may be, and often are, the victims of misplaced confidence, and may be forced to lie and deceive.

It must be evident that undeveloped spirits who come from a Purgatorial world to teach us earthly wisdom, must often be less capable of doing so than embodied spirits who, living in a physical world, use with modesty that truth and reason which are given to them.

Moreover, those souls which, apart from divine desires, leave the body and associate with spirits, generally encounter those no better, and often worse than themselves, and are thus seduced to evil, and this even by spirits assuming the form of angels of light ; hence mediumship is a dangerous possession, and is only for those whose lives are pure, unselfish, and holy. But mediums whose lives are pure, unselfish, and holy are saints, and may sometimes reveal to men the wisdom of angels.

All that is claimed by mediums is the reverse of the powers claimed by the adept. The medium is *negative* but the adept is *positive*.

The oriental adept refuses to submit his body to the use of others, but so brings his body under the control of his own soul that he can project his soul and spirit, and, while living on this earth, act as if he were a disembodied spirit. Hence the adept can consciously see the minds of others. He can act by his soul force on external spirits. He can, it is said, accelerate the growth of plants and quench fire, and, like Daniel, subdue ferocious wild beasts. He can send his soul to a distance, and there not only read the thoughts of others, but speak to and touch these distant objects ; and not only so, but he can exhibit to his distant friends his spiritual body in the exact likeness of that of the flesh.

Moreover, as the adept acts by the power of his spirit, and over other spirits, he can, as a unitive force, create out of the surrounding multiplex atmosphere, the likeness of any physical object, or he can command physical objects to come into his presence.

These statements will not be credited by those ignorant of such things, but Oriental Adepts assert that these statements are absolute facts, and, knowing what I do of mesmerism, I can believe these statements. Granting that they may be facts, the so-called adept is still open to wide delusions, and as his aim usually is only to obtain power for its own sake, his life may become one of hard self-worship or devilry.

Mesmerism, now called hypnotism, as being within the reach of scientific experimentation, throws great light on occult phenomena.

The mesmeric, sensitive as a clairvoyant, can see the thoughts of others, and can read print in closed spaces; and the mesmeriser can at times order the entranced soul or spirit of the sensitive to travel to a distance, and then not only see those there present, but touch them.

The mesmeric sensitive thus resembles the medium in so far as she is passive, but she differs both from the medium and from the adept in this, that her soul or spirit is under the control of a being living on this earth—instead of being under the control of foreign spirits, as with mediums, or under the control of his own spirit, as with the adepts. As the adept can only obtain spiritual power after the severest discipline and self-control, he becomes thus trained to control his spiritual desires. But should he fail to do so, and become the victim of selfish desires, he becomes an evil magician, and then his fall is as that of Lucifer.

Mesmeric healing appears to me to be of three degrees :—

1st. As mere "animal magnetism" the diseased or negative subject by receiving the positive magnetism of the operator is strengthened.

2nd. The magnetiser, by using will force, can so act on the brain and mind of the sensitive as to alter molecular action, and thus heal disease.

3rd. The wholesome, pure, and benevolent man or woman, by simply placing the hands on the patient, and calmly desiring the blessing of God, would seem to become sometimes as a medium for the transmission of spiritual benevolence.

The power of oriental adepts to heal diseases rests, it is said, chiefly on the power of the will, but the power of Christ and His disciples to heal disease was the power of the love and will of God.

The Christian Alchemists asserted that their power to convert the lower metals into gold, and to create precious stones, consisted in the use as a basis of that ultimate unitive in matter which was reached by a series of successive fermentation, by which the ultimate spirit was distilled; and so, also, they asserted that the regenerated and sanctified body, soul, and spirit of man, were also thus reached by a successive series of deaths and resurrections.

Jesus of Nazareth being filled with the Holy Spirit became the Christ, the only-begotten and well-beloved Son of God, *par excellence*, the complete and perfect spiritual Man, and thus the Saviour of the souls of those who, regarding Him as the Way, the Truth, and the Life, become *one* with Him as He is one with the Father.

This position Christ obtained through perfect submission to the will of God, and He thereby obtained spiritual gifts and powers beyond all possibility to soul or human force.

If we become one with Him as He was one with God, then we shall also, after a measure, possess like gifts.

Those saints who entirely surrendered self to the the will of God, being filled with the Spirit, became luminous, healed diseases, and wrought miracles.

The oriental adept sometimes "scales the heavens by violence," and at other times by the pure desire of the soul, but the saints ascended to heaven, as did Elijah, by the power of the love of God.

The sacrifice of Christ is self-sacrifice, and is the sacrifice of the soul and body to the will and love of God, and this is the only true method of salvation by Christ.

Thus religion and morality are nothing more and nothing less than love to God and love to man. Or the spirit of the Son seeking the spirit of God the Father, and "as the Father worketh hitherto," so we desire now to work.

No form of Christianity can be true which ignores or under-estimates the deep significance of the miracles of Christ, for such miracles are inseparable from the truly divine life, and exhibit the divine possibilities contained in the triune manhood.

This is Theosophy, that "the Will of God be done on Earth, as in Heaven."

By miracles, I mean the power of the One Spirit to supplant all secondary forces, whether the spirit manifest itself as when the Spirit of God moving on the face of the waters called life into existence and the earth out of chaos; or when the Spirit of Christ healed diseases and cast out demons, or changed water into wine, or passed into a closed chamber, "the door being shut," or when the spirit of man, when like Christ, it does like works, because He is with His saints to the end of the world.

The diagram I now submit, the initial hint of which I got from my late friend, John Dove, represents my views as to the difference between soul and spirit, and the gradations of each. It will be observed that, in occult language, "as above so below," there are four corresponding gradations of Soul and Spirit, and the diagram represents the Evolution of Soul into the higher Spirit :—

⁎ The Holy Spirit of the Lord

A | The Spirit of Man at one with the will of God
B | The Spirit acts with Divine Reason
C | The Spirit Vision, or Clairvoyance, or Intuition
D | The Spirit Revery or Delusion.

X————————•————————X   The River of Oblivion.

d | The Soul's Revery or day dreaming
c | The Imagination
b | The Rational Soul
a | The Soul or will force

X X Represents the middle wall of partition—the river of oblivion, which separates the soul sphere from the spirit sphere.

• Represents the soul in a position of equipoise or *oblivious* sleep, placed in "the valley of the *shadow* of death."

d Represents the soul in a state of revery—liable to delusion, or "Electro-Biology."

D Represents the soul on first awaking in the spirit sphere of revery, mesmeric or other, namely, in the condition easily imposed on by soul force; in a purgatorial state of hallucination, and prone to impose on others. It is from this region, I believe, that for the most part, come those spirits which haunt our promiscuous *séances*. They descend through the narrow way and "biologise" the mediums who are in a condition of soul revery at d.

C This represents the position of the clairvoyant spirit, but still within the influence of the corresponding region of soul imagination at c, namely, the

Image-ation, or imagination, or creative power of the soul. C being the creative power of the spirit. The soul imagination creates images, but in the imagination or creative power of the spirit these images become objective realities.

B This is the position of spiritual reason and spiritual knowledge and power.

A This is the position where the spirit, being beyond earth and human reason, has become a perfect unity, at one with the Holy Spirit of the Lord, and in perfect subjection to the will of God. Its utterances being, "Thus saith the Lord."

The evolution of the Soul or reasoning faculty being thus through dreaming to more and more profound entrancement in the Spirit.

III.—SPIRITUAL DYNAMICS.*

FIFTY-FIVE years ago, at Edinburgh, in the year 1839, I made the acquaintance of the late Mr. John Dove, subsequently sub-editor of *The Builder*, and was by him first introduced to the marvels of mesmerism and clairvoyance.

Mr. Dove was for thirty years an incessant experimental student of alchemy and its cognate mystical co-relations.

He was the most indefatigable and strongly enthusiastic man I have ever known; but it was not difficult to discover how one of so determined, persistent, and impetuous a will should have made few friends and retained still fewer; and thus it was that for many years I was almost his only visitor.

I have always believed that if Mr. Dove had to his unequalled powers of persistent experimentation, and his wonderful faculty of comparison and generalisation, superadded worldly wisdom, and the art of lucid and abridged statement, and had soared with a less transcendental ambition, and turned his great analytical faculties to the discoveries of science in the ordinary current manner, he might have become the greatest chemist of the age.

* Read before the Cambridge University Psychological Society, November 20th, 1879.

It was under the tuition of this man that my mind was first opened to the conception of that mystery of nature called "animal magnetism," with its phenomena of trance and rigidity of the limbs, and total indifference to the tortures of the body, as applied by inquiring, and sometimes ferocious sceptics—that condition which may be described as "being dead in the flesh but alive in the spirit," when the realisation of mind acting independently of the human organs of sense is manifested, as in clairvoyance, when the bodily and mental secrets of those present can be seen and revealed by the ecstatic, when objects miles and hundreds of miles distant are seen and described, when not only the secrets of those present but the worldly acts of those who have departed this life are made known, and when sometimes the secrets hidden in the womb of fate are foretold.

In those days the clairvoyante always spoke in her own name, in the first or third person singular. Her expressions were, " I see so and so," or, " She says so and so "; this third person seeming to indicate the other, not her conscious self, on the plane of this earth, namely, the new, or exalted, or spiritual counterpart of the earth man. The clairvoyante in those early days never spoke of being controlled by individuals or *bands* of foreign spirits, but professed to utter the revelations of her inner and secret spiritual nature and vision.

It must not be thought from these observations that I deny that evil, or fallen, or earth-bound spirits may infest the bodies of those physically, mentally, or morally diseased ; or that, on rare occasions, angelic spirits may not whisper to our souls. On the contrary, I believe, as the Bible and other histories teach, that a large proportion of what is called insanity is, as the victims themselves persistently declare, the result of demoniacal possession by unclean spirits ; while, on the other hand, I believe that a large proportion of all instructive and grand and noble and creative thoughts, comes to our soul or spirit through its unconscious communion with angelic intelligence, or through the spirits of those who live in spirit and in truth.

The late Sir James Simpson, the renowned Edinburgh physician, and the late Sir William Hamilton, the profound metaphysician, took great interest in Mr. Dove's mesmeric experiments. Dr. Simpson was in the habit afterwards of ridiculing the subject, having doubtless before his eyes the fate of the good Dr. Elliotson, who having introduced mesmerism practically to his patients at University College Hospital, was, as the reward of his benevolent work, execrated by the profession and expelled from the hospital, while his practice fell from about £5,000 a year to about £1,000 ; and all this because he desired to impart a knowledge regarding a mystery in human nature which he *knew* to be of transcendant importance in the diagnosis and treatment of disease. And now in these latter days hypnotism is the fashion.

For some ten years subsequent to the above events I had little opportunity of pursuing my observations in mesmerism and its kindred subjects, but in 1855 Mr. Home arrived in London, and my avidity for that form of psychology known as Spiritualism became profoundly awakened.

A knowledge of mesmerism not only predisposes the mind to a ready acceptance of many of the phenomena called spiritual, but throws a light on these phenomena which cannot be otherwise obtained.

In the presence of Home, hands of human form and character became materialised, and made themselves known both to sight and feeling; and I can never forget the overwhelming sensations I experienced on first seeing and touching these hands — warm, sensitive, *detached* hands — which grasped my hand with the perfect reality of human hands, and yet dissolved from the grasp as no human hands could do. On awaking next morning after the night which followed my first experience, I had some difficulty in persuading myself that the whole had not been a dream.

Shortly after my first introduction to the mystery of spiritual phenomena, I retired from further active investigation of the subject, in the belief that it was one accompanied by great moral, if not physical danger; but my interest became again excited when the Davenport Brothers arrived in London, and demonstrated the fact that no form of material bonds could resist the disintegrating force of magical power.

I readily admit that here, as elsewhere, fraudulent imitations sometimes took place so closely simulating the reality as to deceive all except those who, by repeated tests and crucial experiments *know* that there is a spiritual force exhibited in the presence of certain human beings, which, being the ultimate force in nature, can analyse and dissolve and supersede all *secondary* chemical and mechanical forces.

The Dialectic Society, by a Committee, investigated the claims of Spiritualism in 1870, and invited those who had experience to give evidence. I was also invited to attend some of the sittings of the committee, but I was never called upon to give evidence.

At one of these meetings I met Mr. Serjeant Cox* for the first time, and volunteered to him the opinion I had formed that as man was potentially a spiritual being, the phenomena called spiritual might come from a force in the possession of some one bodily present at a *séance*, quite independent of the aid of the spirits of *departed* human beings.

---

* This paper was read and printed before the death of Mr. Serjeant Cox.

Mr. Serjeant Cox expressed himself much interested in this view, and two years afterwards published his important and interesting book in illustration of *the psychic force*.

The views I hold, however, on this subject differ from those held by Mr. Cox as expressed in his writings; for while he held that *all* the so-called spiritual phenomena *are* produced by the psychic force of human beings in the body, I, on the contrary, hold that all phenomena within the capability of departed human spirits *can* be produced by the spirits of human beings not departed, but that, as presented to us, some of the phenomena are from the one source and some from the other; that this psychic force can be exercised by some beings in the body, but that much more easily and frequently the souls of departed human beings can and do exercise the same force.

Again I ceased actively to occupy myself with Spiritualism until the spring of 1877, when Slade arrived in London.

I paid three visits to Slade, and obtained about twenty experiments, and became absolutely convinced that in his presence writing could be obtained in closed spaces, access to which by human hands or instruments was an absolute impossibility.

Thus it was that when Lankester dragged Slade into the police-court, I at once came forward and became his bail for £100, and afterwards appeared as a witness in his defence.

I stated in court that I would, in order to save time, base my evidence entirely on one experiment.

My statement was that I took one out of many slates lying on a side table before me. Having taken this slate in hand, I would not permit Slade to touch it. I examined it for a considerable time on both sides. It was a dry, dusty, new school slate, without the slightest trace of writing on its surface. I then took a small fragment of slate pencil and laid it on the table, and covered it with my slate. I then seized both of Slade's legs between mine, and both his hands in mine, and having rested my elbow on the slate, I said to Slade, "I am ready; now write." Instantly I heard a sound as of rapid, energetic writing with a slate pencil, and then three raps to indicate that the message was finished. I released Slade's hands, and carefully raising the slate from the table, I found a message clearly written in strong dusty slate writing, composed of about twenty words, and containing five of my family names, and a message urging two of my sceptical brothers to investigate the subject. I added that the table on the top of which the slate rested was a solid, hard wood table, and that physical access to the under surface of my slate was, as it lay on the table, an impossibility.

This experiment, together with many others I had, enabled me in court solemnly to assert that I could not be more certain of my own existence than I was that the writing on the slate could not possibly have come through human hands or instruments.

The theory I formed at the time, but afterwards modified, regarding the production of slate writing, was that it was *probably* in most instances produced by the soul or spirit of Slade himself, but unknown to Slade; and it may, perhaps, assist the sceptic to comprehend how such things are possible if I offer the following attempt at an explanation.

We all know that the magnet can repel and attract, and elevate from the ground in opposition to the laws of inertia and gravity, a bit of iron.

This, although the most commonplace of experiments, and one known to man for thousands of years, is yet, as to its meaning, altogether beyond the comprehension of the most profound students of magnetism. It is a mystery of mysteries, and yet it is universally known and believed.

It is incomprehensible how one bit of iron can attract and draw through space another bit of iron without any conceivable attachment or physical communication.

Why, then, do all human beings believe in a fact which is not only incomprehensible, but, abstractedly considered, an impossibility?

The reply is, we believe it because we *know* it to be a fact. Exactly so; and the initiated believe in spiritual phenomena for exactly the same reason—they *know* them to be facts—with the absolute conviction of their own existence.

If, then, the magnet, contrary to the laws of inertia and gravity, can move a bit of iron in a closed space, to and fro and up and down, why should it seem impossible that the human mind, or will, or soul, or spirit should, without the intervention of human hands, move in like manner, but with intelligence, a bit of slate pencil, and write intelligent sentences? If the soul, when free and clairvoyant, can see without eyes, why should it not be able to *act* without hands?

The phenomena of magnetism and slate-writing are both equally wonderful; the only difference is, that slate-writing not being at all times obtainable, like magnetism, is more *extra*-ordinary.

I felt so intensely earnest in my convictions regarding the genuineness of the Slade performance, and the profound bearing it had on the laws of mind and matter, that I felt I could have submitted to any martyrdom in its defence, and, therefore, I never hesitated to appear as a witness in defence of Slade; although knowing that ninety-nine persons in the hundred regarding him as a common impostor, I could not appear at a police court publicly in his defence without incurring great professional risks.

The result was as I anticipated. I was abused and denounced in many quarters; I received many insulting anonymous letters, some friends quarrelled with me, and my professional receipts began and continued to decline.

But there is a grand promise by *the Master*, that no one who forsakes friends and worldly goods for the truth, but shall even here receive an ample recompense.

So it has been with myself. For one friend I have lost I have gained many better friends, and even my worldly prosperity has been indirectly through these friends increased; and not only so, but my professional reputation, apart from practice, has been greatly increased also, indirectly through Spiritualism; for there came to me in a mysterious manner, indirectly in connection with the Slade trial, an idea which I conveyed to the profession through the London press, which communication showered upon me immediately in reply about four hundred letters of thanks and congratulations from medical men in all parts of England.

Reverting to what I have said regarding the different views held by Mr. Serjeant Cox and myself on this subject, I here observe that man is equally a spiritual being whether his body be alive or dead, and that the spirits of certain human beings may leave the body in sleep or during entrancement, or during mere "absence of mind," when the *double* may become visible; while other human beings exists who can, by practice of will-force, project their souls or spirits externally to the body, and operate on matter at a distance by what is called magical power.

If we can realise these statements and understand how the spirit is the man, and the body a mere machine of a temporary nature by which matter is brought in contact with matter in the ordinary course of nature, and that matter itself is only a form assumed by force, we have the key to all the phenomena called spiritual, whether occurring through the agency of foreign spirits operating through mediums, or by the will force of positive magicians, or by the *pneumic* force of ecstatics.

Human beings uninfluenced by agnosticism almost without exception believe that after the death of their bodies they exist as intelligent operating spiritual beings. If so, wherein lies the difficulty of believing that such beings should on rare occasions walk the earth, and through the agency of a medium's body operate in spirit circles?

The orthodox doctrine is that the spirits of the departed are confined either in heaven or hell, and cannot re-visit the earth. But the Christian teaching is, that evil spirits operate with demoniacs, and that good spirits and angels at rare intervals also re-appear on this earth.

I say such high spirits are described as rarely appearing on this earth, and therefore I believe, if spirits they are, which haunt our promiscuous spirit circles, they must be idle, foolish, or purgatorial spirits for the most part.

Once realise that the spirit is the man and the body a mere temporary appearance, and that what we call matter is only form assumed by force, and all the phenomena called spiritual can be understood, and the foundation of a true experimental psychology is established.

Let us review the order of these phenomena, and on the above theory attempt a possible solution of the problems.

1. Mesmeric power can be demonstrated to act on sensitives who will obey from a *distance* the will of the operator, thus demonstrating the action of mind on mind at a distance.

2. The very common experiment of blindfolding certain individuals and then touching them with one finger, or sometimes willing them without contact, and thus compelling them to act according to your *secret thoughts*, demonstrates again the silent action of mind on mind, and mind on the bodies of second persons.

3. Audible raps by invisible agencies are produced on tables, etc., in the presence of psychics, and thereby spirit messages spelt out.

SPIRITUAL DYNAMICS.

4. So, then, we can understand that it is but a step further to move tables and articles of furniture in the presence of psychics by the forces of attraction and repulsion guided by intelligence, as possessed by the spirits either of the living or the departed.

5. From the moving of furniture it is easy to proceed a step further and produce direct spirit-writing in closed spaces by the operation of attraction and repulsion, guided by intelligence, or by the will of foreign spirits who may be present.

6. Everyone experienced in these phenomena has both seen and felt human-like materialised hands—some soft, some hard, some dry, and others moist, some warm, others cold.

7. If hands can be materialised by spirit force, it is only one step further to materialise the semblance of an entire human body, and accordingly such forms have hundreds of times been produced (although this is a production many times more difficult than the production of hands), and have in many respects acted as human beings in the flesh. Such forms may be sometimes only animated automata, or they may be forms inhabited by the souls of living or departed human beings, or they may be merely masks or simulacra.

These materialisations, however, are in dark rooms, often unconsciously simulated by entranced, or sometimes fraudulent, mediums.

8. A form presenting itself as any known individual departed this life may be a mere simulacrum, it being as easy for spirits to produce the likeness of any desired form as it is for the actor or painter in this life to do so; and more so, for spirits have access to all kinds of information. And hence the identity of personating spirits cannot easily, if at all, be proved logically to third persons, but can only be instinctively perceived to be true by those to whom the communication is directly given, my own opinion being that not one materialisation in twenty is the individuality it pretends to be.

To comprehend how spiritual materialisations are possible, we must reflect on the fact that all substances are composed of a few elements, and that those elements exist in the air and moisture and earth in contact with us.

There was a time when this planet was an incandescent mass, which, as it cooled, became a globe of crystalline rocks, surrounded probably by hot steam, which ultimately became condensed as water. From the action of this water on the solid rocks, and with the assistance of the atmosphere, a soil was produced, out of which soil, by a process beyond all natural knowledge, sprang plants and ultimately animals.

If so, then we have *inorganic* substances as the matrix out of which spirit created *living* and organic beings. We know that the air plant flourishes without any soil, and that gold-fish flourish in water without visible organic food; and if so, it is not difficult to believe that Louise Lateau, of Belgium, or Miss Fansha,* of New York, might live for years without organic nourishment.

We know that the seeds of plants have the power of creating from inorganic elements at a certain rate of time, flowers and fruits unlike the original seed. That, for instance, the seed of a rose can, out of clay and fetid manure, create a rose of ravishing fragrance and beauty.

If seeds have such a power, is it impossible to conceive that the God-like human spirit, when it has "*faith as a grain of mustard seed*," may have also a creative power, and create from the elements around us the semblance of human hands, faces, and forms?

9. Certain individuals, as Mr. Home for instance, at times are possessed of the power of elongating their bodies some inches. We may conceive of this if we reflect that *cold* indiarubber cannot be elongated, but if warmed, that is, if made subject to vibration, it can. This fact in itself is almost as mysterious as the powers of the magnet to attract and repel iron. Thus it is analogously with the human body. In its normal condition it grows at a slow rate, but under the analysing, dissolving, and expanding influence of the ultimate force in nature, spirit, such acts can be

---

* See *Spiritualist*, Oct. 13, 1878.

accelerated. The rapid growth of plants, as exhibited by Indian jugglers, is an insoluble mystery to our jugglers, and may be a further illustration of a like spirit power.

10. The power of will or mesmeric force, or spiritual force, or prayer, to heal disease, is easily understood on the dynamic theory of matter.*

All form is the result of given forces. That which becomes deformed or diseased, does so either because the animal force is deficient or deranged, hence all which is required to heal is that a normal force displace the defective or irregular force. Harmony is thus produced in the molecular position and construction of the body, and a cure is the result.

11. The alchemist asserts that the base metallic lead may be converted into the royal gold, and that the man of clay may be transformed into the divine man by the action of spiritual force ; and this we can as readily believe as we can that natural forces, being the machinery used by the Divine Mind, such forces can be accentuated as, we say, occurs in the working of miracles. For miracle is only the accentuation of the ordinary forces in nature, as when water was converted into wine or the blind into seeing eyes by the power of spirit to dissolve and re-arrange the molecules of matter.

---

* *The World Dynamical and Immaterial*, by R. S. Wyld, LL.D. Oliver and Boyd.

12. The passage of matter through matter is of all spiritual phenomena the most difficult to realise. Moreover, being instantaneous, it has never been actually *seen* in action. Christians believe in Christ having so acted when He appeared "in the midst of His disciples, the doors being shut"; and so also with Peter when he passed unfettered out of prison. And Spiritualists can enumerate not less than a thousand instances where books and other solid substances have entered closed chambers.

The dynamic explanation is that there is no such thing as solid matter, but only a certain proximity of atoms, or centres of force, held in position by attraction, and that by an expansive, spiritual or centrifugal force these atoms can be so separated as to admit of the passage of other so-called solid substances. Atoms if placed in a like electrical condition, would repel each other; and as spirits assert that magnetism is their motive-power, we can realise how the molecules of so-called solid matter may expand and contract instantaneously.

Let * represent a molecule of so-called solid matter; it is conceivable that the atoms of the molecule might be so polarised as to fly asunder, the result being to separate them thus ⁂—and so rendering opaque, solid matter transparent and patulous. But this is further illustrated in my paper on Matter.

We know that solid ice, by the application of a

force called *heat*, which is only certain vibrations, can be dissolved into liquid water; and we know by an increased amount of heat force, that is, by more rapid vibrations, this water may be dissipated into *invisible* steam. Apply an expanding force which can, like spirit, act instantaneously, and the magical performance of matter instantaneously passing through matter is so far explained. " In a moment, in the twinkling of an eye, all can be changed."

13. Certain individuals, mediums, magicians, and ecstatics have been levitated from the earth to various elevations, as witnessed by many in England, America, and India, and as is also well known to the historians of the Romish Church.

Masses of clouds, that is, masses of watery vapour, float in the sky, contrary to the law of gravity, being probably electrically repelled from the earth, and he who has observed large birds, such as ravens, floating for miles without almost moving a muscle—although he knows that this is generally explained by the supposed correlation between the air currents and the steering power of the bird—has yet suggested to his mind that the electric state of the bird in relation to the earth may be the true explanation of how a heavy bird can float in air independent of visible muscular action.

Thus when levitation takes place with human beings, although it may be from the assistance of foreign spirits, yet the more likely explanation is that the body and the earth being in a like magnetic condition, the one repels the other ; or, as with saintly ecstatics, it may be described as the "elevating, or centrifugal, or radiating force of Divine Love." I should add that the power to float in the air possessed by certain Indian adepts is by Hindu philosophers attributed to the power of the will to alter magnetic conditions.

14. The highest manifestation of spirit force is illustrated in those who, living a pure and holy live, do in ecstatic prayer not only rise from the ground but become effulgent, for "when the eye is single the whole body is full of light"; but of this I have spoken more abundantly in my paper on the Christian Saints.

Spiritual phenomena demonstrate that there is within man's body, and, when that body dies, external to that body, an intelligent spiritual force, which can directly by will-power, or indirectly by controlling other spirits, move without the intervention of a visible organisation material substance, and thus in five minutes refute the materialistic talk and ignorance of three thousand years.

But Spiritualism has its evil as well as its true side.

It is a great evil when ignorant, or foolish, or idle, or selfish people make it a subject of amusement. It is a great evil when these people receive the vapid, or commonplace, or inflated verbiage of some "inspirational medium," as not only a guide for their lives, but as a revelation of celestial truth, or of a new religion higher than that we have in the teachings and life of Christ.

Spiritual phenomena demonstrate that the miraculous history in our Bible is consistent with known facts. They demonstrate that the spirit of man can act on matter irrespective of a physical organisation, and that, therefore, the spirit lives and acts independent of the organic body. And they show that there exists in man a spiritual nature, which proves him to be not only an immortal being, but capable of coming into spiritual relationship with God.

Thus spiritual phenomena provide us with a key to the only true psychology, an experimental knowledge of the nature and powers of the human soul, and show *how* the salvation of that soul is the ultimate psychological fact.

For myself, I believe that the phenomena and philosophy of Spiritualism are destined to remould science, philosophy, psychology, and *dogmatic* theology from their very foundation, by showing how a spiritual and divine intelligent force constitutes the essence of all things.

The power to move matter by will, and without the intervention of mechanism, demonstrates the intelligent spiritual nature of man; while the spiritual phenomena which occur in the presence of believers can, in five minutes, refute the material philosophy of thousands of years.

Beyond this, the higher philosophy of Spiritualism reveals the structure of the human soul, and thus becomes the only scientific psychology.

The mere knowledge of the facts of Spiritualism cannot save the soul; but true Spiritualism can show *how* the soul is saved as a psychological and physiological fact.

When Spiritualists proceed farther and speak of Spiritualism as a new religion, they utter that which to me has no meaning. The essence of all religion is one and identical. It is the cry of the soul after its hidden centre and its Lord—as the child cries for its mother, "as the hart panteth after the water-brooks."

There may be those who in Spiritualism find a new sect, or a new superstition; but to discover a new religion would be as impossible as to find a new God.

Spiritualism, as it demonstrates man to be a spirit, at the same time demonstrates the fact of a spiritual life hereafter. But the immense majority of human beings require no such demonstration, as ninety-nine in a hundred instinctively believe and are assured that there is a future life.

Swedenborg and Spiritualism certainly show good reasons for believing that our future life will be the counterpart of this life, and that we shall occupy a position there in exact relation to our works here.

But Christianity also teaches the same when it says, " Shall not the Lord render to every man according to his works?" and "One star differeth from another star in glory," and "To whom much is given, of him shall much be required," and "He who knew not shall be beaten with few stripes."

Moreover, Modern Spiritualism cannot be a *new* religion, inasmuch as the whole Bible is full of Spiritualism, and the Roman Church has never ceased to exemplify this in the lives of her saints.

Protestantism has laughed to scorn these spiritual claims of the Romish Church, but modern Spiritualism proves that these claims are founded on facts.

The Romish St. Teresa was a saint and prophetess, but so also was the Lutheran Seeress of Prevorst. The spiritual teachings of both are identical, and their lives were equally pure and given to God; but St. Teresa worshipped more the Supreme, while the Seeress gave herself chiefly to spiritual philosophy and to the benefaction of the afflicted.

The simple doctrine of the love of God and the love of man taught by Christ as the sum and substance of all religion and morality cannot be surpassed, and can be understood by all; but the hidden and esoteric doctrine of Christ can be understood by those only who hold the mystical key, and in this respect the Romish Church is wiser than Protestantism. I admit this; but let no one suppose from this admission that a true Theosophist, to whom had been revealed the secret of the Logos, could ever find it necessary to enter that Church, or that he could regard, except with horror, his subjugation to a priesthood which, asserting that it holds the keys of the kingdom of heaven, too often, alas, has used those keys only to shut the door, "neither going in itself, nor suffering them who are entering to go in."

The true Theosophist requires no such priesthood, but for him it is sufficient, when he discovers that all his past life he has been feeding on the husks which the swine do eat, to say, "I will arise and go to my Father," for he then experiences "the glorious liberty of the children of God." Even the Popish St. Teresa, when in her highest ecstasies she became united to Christ, and thus found that she was one with God, shows the non-necessity of all priestly interference; and she could then, in the magnificent language of St. Paul, say, "Neither death, nor life, nor angels, nor principalities, nor powers, nor things present, nor things to come, nor height, nor depth, nor any other creature, shall be able to separate us from the love of God, which is in Christ Jesus our Lord."

That spiritual phenomena are real I know as certainly as I know that I exist. In this paper I therefore assume their reality.*

Should the sceptic say that I should demonstrate the facts before I construct my theory, I reply that no

---

* In the library of the Spiritual Alliance, 2, Duke Street, Charing Cross, the inquirer will find the records of thousands of spiritual facts contained in several hundred volumes.

amount of written or oral evidence can convince the obstinate sceptic, that is, one whose organisation renders spiritual vision impossible. But this I can promise him, that no man of average common sense, common instincts, and common honesty, could radically or thoroughly investigate the subject by reading, by conversations with those who know, and by *persistent* experimental investigation in spite of many disappointments, and fail at last to know, as I do, that spiritual phenomena are as real as his own life.

The laborious student of this most deeply interesting but intricate and occult subject, will discover that there is a form of Spiritualism which, while dealing with a low class of spirits for foolish or wicked purposes, is the forbidden necromancy or witchcraft. This is a form of Spiritualism which might convert this earth into a pandemonium by the demoniacal possession of human beings, a condition of the world which existed in the days of Christ, "who came to save the world by destroying the works of the Devil." Another form of Spiritualism is soul-force and that is in union with Spirit, magic—which may be used for good purposes, or may be perverted into dangerous and demoniacal power. A third form of Spiritualism believes in our communion with angels and saints. But there is yet a fourth form of Spiritualism, which is the voice of God illuminating the *centre* of the soul, and this is altogether holy and divine.

IV.—MAN AS A SPIRIT;

AND SPIRITUAL PHENOMENA AS PRODUCED BY THE SPIRITS OF THE LIVING.*

WE are often told that in Spiritualism our great first duty is to accumulate facts. So, indeed, it is; but in this paper I shall, being thoroughly satisfied of the reality of the facts, take them for granted, and attempt to maintain a theory as to their nature.

Briefly stated, my theory is this. Man is a spirit; therefore, if the phenomena we call Spiritual are produced by spirits, there is no reason why the operating spirits should not be those of the living beings present. I wish it to be distinctly kept in mind that I do not say that all the phenomena we are acquainted with *are* so produced; I simply say and believe that most of the phenomena we have yet obtained *might* be produced by the spirits of the living.

Secondly, I say that inasmuch as we, as spirits, know we are present, but have no absolute proof that spirits of the departed are present, the presumption is that our spirits, known to be present, are the operators.

Thirdly, The presence of a medium is almost

---

*Read before the British Association of Spiritualists, December 10th, 1877.

always necessary to the production of the phenomena, —therefore the presumption is that the spirit of the medium is the chief operator, and yet after further experience, I am persuaded that most of the phenomena called Spiritual are produced by spiritual beings outside ourselves.

One day, in the year 1853, I met an old artistic and mesmeric friend, Mr. Collin, who, knowing me to be interested in psychological phenomena, asked me if I had seen Mr. Home, the wonderful American medium, who had just arrived in London. I replied that I had not, when he said, " Then lose no time in making his acquaintance, for you will find that Spiritualism is a fact, and that it beats mesmerism into fits." He then narrated to me what he had seen and felt, namely, the production of spirit hands, which to the evidence of the senses were identical with human hands.

I replied, that I had believed in mesmerism since the year 1839, and was therefore mentally prepared to receive almost any mystery; but he must excuse me if I declined to believe in his narrative until I had witnessed the facts with my own eyes.

Mr. Collin admitted that I was quite right, but at the same time assured me that I had only to witness the phenomena to be at once convinced of the solid reality of the facts.

A few days later I had the good fortune to secure a sitting with Mr. Home, when, sure enough, in bright gas-light, a hand became visible, and grasped my hand with a reality "as palpable as this I wear," compelling an instantaneous belief, Mr. Home being about ten feet distant from me, and all other hands at the table being joined together.

Mr. Home afterwards passed into a trance, and said to me: "I see Isabella," a cousin of mine, who had shortly before passed into spirit life. That he saw Isabella mentally I felt convinced, because he gave me the most positive evidence, by mimicking her gestures and actions, which in one minute detail I have never seen repeated in any other woman. Being well acquainted with the phenomena of mind-reading and clairvoyance, I at once, in my own mind, secretly concluded that Home was a clairvoyant; but no sooner had this idea entered my mind, than Mr. Home replied to my thought by saying, "You think this is mind-reading, but it is not; I *see* Isabella." I felt that I could not have obtained a better proof that the vision was one of mind-reading, and yet not necessarily so, for Home might at one and the same time be able to read thought and to see spirits.

I did not at that time see how my theory applied to the production of palpable hands, but this revelation so astonished me, that, when I awoke the following morning, I had some difficulty in believing that the whole had not been a dream.

Home, as we know, on certain occasions became

elongated several inches, but it is much easier to believe that his own spirit, the master of his own body, exercised this disintegrating act, than that a foreign spirit performed the operation.

Home also floated in the air, but we do not find any necessity to call in the aid of foreign spirits to accomplish this feat. Home might have been repelled from the earth, just as two bodies similarly electrified repel each other; or his irradiating or levitating spirit may have rendered his body specifically lighter than the atmosphere; and this view I would rather suggest, as the motion, of Home floating through the upper part of the room, and in and out of window, had a close resemblance to the gliding, floating actions of the fish in water, moving here and there as by volition.

I did not at that time continue my investigations, because events occurred which showed to me that the subject was one the investigation of which might involve terrible consequences.

Some years later Mrs. Hardinge came to London, and delivered those powerful orations which purported to be from the dictations of wise spirits from the spirit-land.

Here again I received the impression that these orations were not the dictation of departed spirits, but the improvisations of her own partially entranced, and therefore clairvoyant spirit.

I had on former occasions seen very plain, common,

and uninteresting women, when entranced, become at once, as it were, transfigured in both mind and body, and speak and act in a manner far beyond their natural powers; and why should not Emma Hardinge, with her educated and powerful mind, in her partially entranced condition, deliver orations transcending her natural abilities?

Mr. Dove and I urged this view on Mrs. Hardinge, and she admitted that she believed it might often be so, at least to some extent.

These views I expressed at the meeting held in the Harley Street Rooms, to discuss the question of Spiritualism, and Mr. Coleman has printed them in his interesting little book, *The History of Spiritualism in England*. It was objected to my views that communications were received on subjects either forgotten, and therefore not in our minds, or on subjects beyond our knowledge. To this my answer was, that to the entranced and clairvoyant spirit, all minds and books were open for inspection and instruction; and that, although subjects had faded from our memories, there yet remained their impress on the tablets of our minds, or their aura adhering to us.

Afterwards the Davenport brothers arrived and astonished us, and asserted that their bonds were untied by spirits, and that spirit hands assisted them. No doubt the Davenports were released from the most perfect tying, and no doubt spirit hands and arms were visibly multiplied; but I said, if departed spirits can do this work, why not spirits present in our own bodies?

Regarding this theory I received what seemed to me a strong confirmation, when on asking Mr. Everett if he could give me any idea how he was liberated from the most perfectly secure handcuffs, as applied by the most experienced police-sergeants, he replied that he did not know how it was, but that at the moment the act took place he felt himself entranced This confirmed me in my belief that the handcuffs were removed by the mechanical dexterity of his own spirit. Although his entrancement might have been a necessity for the intervention of spirits.

Lastly arrived Slade, and, with regard to slate-writing, I would observe that there is no order of spiritual phenomena which impresses me more powerfully. Slade and his slate-writing were to me objects of absorbing interest. All was done in the light, and above board. The evidence that the writing was produced by a spiritual intelligence, without the intervention of human hands, was overwhelming; and in his presence the materialism of 3,000 years was refuted in five minutes. When, therefore, brutal and intolerant ignorance seized Slade, and dragged him into a police-court, I felt prepared to run any risk and incur any responsibility in his defence.

Slade believed that the writing was chiefly produced by the spirit of his deceased wife; but I believed that it was produced by his own partially entranced spirit. This view has recently received a confirmation by the admission of Mr. Watkins, one of the most surprising of the slate-writers. He is convinced that his own spirit frequently produces the writing, as "he feels a something go out of him as the writing is being done, and a something returning into him as the writing is finished."

But it is objected, how can an ignorant medium write Greek? My reply is, that the *spirit* of the medium may instinctively know Greek, or receive a vision of it, or find it in the brain of those present, or in books.*

Swedenborg tells us that spirits surround themselves with the forms of their affections. If so, why should Slade's spirit not desire and see Greek texts written before the mind's eye.

Let us apply these views to form manifestations. Mrs. Compton, a common, uninteresting woman, goes into a cabinet, and has her *black* dress nailed to the floor of the room. Shortly afterwards out walks the form of a fine young lady dressed in *white*, and, by permission, a bit of the white dress is cut off. The cabinet is now searched, but Mrs. Compton is not

---

* I permit this theory to stand as just written, but I now add that since writing this paper I have come much more round to the theory that most of the mediumistic phenomena of the above kind are produced by foreign spirits.

E

there. The young lady form in white now returns to the cabinet, when shortly afterwards out walks a big man with a beard, which on examination, is found to be not glued to, but *growing* out of the skin of his face. The cabinet is again searched, Mrs. Compton is not there. This bearded man returns to the cabinet, which is again searched, and there sits Mrs. Compton in her *black* dress nailed to the floor, with a bit cut out, which is found exactly to correspond to the bit cut out of the *white* dress of the young lady form.

Here we have an astounding narrative, subjecting the believer to the risk of being shut up as a lunatic ; but what necessity does there exist for calling in the assistance of foreign spirits? Mrs. C. *is* a spirit, and her body belongs to that spirit ; which can by a spiritual chemistry disintegrate it and re-form the materials into any shape which it may desire.

Let us now consider the most recent and the most astounding of all the spiritual phenomena which have occurred in this country.

Dr. Monck is entranced, and in lamp-light ard under the close inspection of Mr. Colley, Mr. Stainton-Moses, Mrs. Going, and others, a mist seems to emanate from his body, near the region of his heart. This mist becomes columnar, it gyrates on its axis, when gradually there is evolved the *solid* frame, make, and character of the deceased Samuel Wheeler. So exactly does this being resemble Samuel Wheeler, in both soul and body, that his oldest friends assert that the figure is absolutely Samuel Wheeler returned in the flesh.

I was not permitted to witness this astounding apparition, and I admit that those who have been so privileged are better entitled than myself to make assertions regarding it. But Mr. Stainton-Moses has recorded his impression that the apparition seemed to him to be a spiritual *automaton*, and this is the view I, in the absence of experience, now hold.

The fact that the figure revealed a secret known only to one individual is, to my mind, no proof of identity, for in the spirit-life the secrets of all hearts are open for inspection. Nor does the absolute conviction of others, as to the identity, convince me. The fact that the figure is sometimes materialised only to the waist, gives one the idea of an automaton; and as to the conviction of friends, we know that spirits can almost " deceive even the elect ; " and have we not, to the minds of accomplished ladies and gentlemen, Arthur Orton presenting himself as Roger Tichborne? but more incredible still, unknown quantities, X.Y.Z., returning from the colonies, and claiming to be lost husbands long reputed as dead, are as such joyfully received by sad and solitary widows. To this it may, indeed, be said that the wish was father to the thought. Such illustrations are, however, not necessary to my theory, for if spirit has, as

Swedenborg says, the power to create physical simulacra, why should it not have the power to create a simulacrum of our most intimate friend?

When I read that on one occasion Dr. Monck awoke out of his trance, and seeing Samuel Wheeler, the two rushed into each other's arms, I was at first puzzled how to reconcile this fact with my theory that the medium must be entranced when the spirit-form is materialised. But on reflection I find that the facts of the double explain this difficulty. A young lady friend of mine on one occasion, as she was proceeding homewards on a cold day, strongly desired to be at home, and in the kitchen warming herself. At that moment two servants in the kitchen saw the handle of the door turn, the door open, and the young lady walk in and warm herself at the fire. They regarded her as identical with their young mistress, even to the minute detail of a pair of new *green* kid gloves; but suddenly she disappeared, and in about a quarter of an hour the young mistress actually appeared in the body, and wearing a pair of *green* kid gloves which she had bought after leaving home. Here we have the double, although the original is awake, and unentranced, beyond the stage it might have been of a mere *absence* of *mind*. But further, we know that there are individuals who can project their double at will in the walking state, and converse with it as with a second distinct individual.

If so, Dr. Monck may be one of those persons, and may have the power of projecting his spirit in the form of himself or of any friend he or his spirit may desire. I am confirmed in this idea by the figure having on one occasion addressed Mr. Wedgwood thus :—" Mr. Wedgwood, I am *Monck's* Samuel Wheeler." To my mind these words do not suggest an independent identity, but rather a subordinate creation or spiritual automaton.

But the Spiritualist replies, it may be with anger, " Why should you deprive us of the greatest comfort of our lives, the belief that we are in daily communion with the spirits of those we loved on earth?" and very far indeed is it from my desire to do so, but I would say that in memory I can love the departed as much as if they were present. Again, it is said the outcome of the science of the nineteenth century is atheism ; but grant the return of one single spirit from the eternal shores, and immortality is at once established. I grant this, and say that the spirits of the departed have a thousand times re-appeared as ghosts, before taking their final leave of this world. Ghost stories are established beyond all question, and the impression produced on the mind by these *spontaneous* ghosts is far more solemn and profound than that which is produced by those spiritually *manufactured* or produced by mediums.

Further, the double demonstrates the existence of

the spirit outside the body, and so far independent of the body. No one, I conceive, could behold a ghost or a double, and not *feel* that man is a spirit, and an immortal being.

Moreover, the entranced man can see without eyes objects five thousand miles distant. He can hear without ears at distances beyond all natural acoustics. He can taste without contact with the food. He can see the past, the present, and the future. To him the secrets of the heart are open. He can heal the diseases of others, and for his own body you may cut it limb from limb, and his spirit will regard the mutilation with entire indifference. You may burn his body with fire, and he will only rejoice in his victory over matter. Is not this a physical demonstration that spirit is independent of matter?— a *unity*, therefore, indivisible, and therefore incapable of decay, and therefore immortal? But I hold that the universal belief in a future state is a demonstration of the fact. All error produces sin and misery, and all truth produces, sooner or later, health and happiness. The belief in a future state is productive of health, strength, and happiness, and therefore I hold that this demonstrates the harmony of this belief with man's nature, and thus demonstrates the reality of a future life. Miracles I define as the dominion of spirit over matter, and thus miracles I hold demonstrate the immortality of the soul. The spiritual man by faith can shut the mouths of lions, and quench the violence of fire; cast out demons, and raise the dead to life. Of matter itself spiritual phenomena go to prove that *per se* it has no existence, matter being only form assumed by force. Granting, for convenience, ultimate atoms, spirit takes these and builds them into any form it may desire or imagine. Just as a certain acid seizing on a certain alkali may produce a *white triangular* crystal, so a stronger acid will displace the weaker, and produce with the same alkali, it may be, a *red hexagonal* crystal, and so on *ad infinitum*.

Read in this light, spiritual chemistry or form materialisings, are profoundly interesting, and go to prove that the spirit of man has, like the Spirit of God, dominion not only over the fowls of the air and the beasts of the field, as Adam had, but over the elements of matter. The idealist excercising his hands can with clay or marble mould or chisel the divinest forms. The spiritual man can create or materialise those forms by the mere force of his spiritual imagination, and the whole universe is only the materialised thoughts of the Divine Mind.

I have spoken much of entrancement, and I may say that my Spiritual theory is mainly founded on that most profoundly interesting fact that man, when he becomes entranced, is not only above and beyond matter, but he becomes the controller of matter. He reveals the hidden angel, and demonstrates that "the kingdom of heaven is within him." I beg the reader's attention to the diagram, page 17.

a to d represents the earthly or soul life. D to A the spirit life. X X represents the middle wall of partition, or river of oblivion, which divides the earth-plane from the spirit-plane.

a represents the ordinary life of self-consciousness and reason and vigilance. d represents the plane of reverie or day-dreaming, or "Electro-biology." • represents the position, the *point* intermediate between the earth or spirit-plane, the point of oblivious sleep. D represents the plane of spirit reverie and spirit-dreaming. This I conceive to be the region of elementary and evil and foolish, or purgatorial spirits —the plane of spirit "Electro-biology," or delusion— the spirits which chiefly infest our dark *séances :* and this may be the position occupied by our spirits when infested in sleep by foul and evil vampires. C represents the position of spiritual lucidity or clairvoyance, or inspirational speaking in company at times with higher departed spirits. B represents a more intense lucidity and clairvoyance ; and here, the spirit sometimes escaping from the influence of the lower plane, is controlled by the "Holy Spirit of the Lord," at A, and hence the form of oracle is "Thus saith the Lord." To this position I conceive St. Paul ascended when he was caught up into the third heaven, and saw things "impossible to utter." A represents the position to which Christ continually ascended, and thus being, as it were, absorbed in God, could say, "I and the Father are one," and became entitled to the name of "the only-begotten and well-beloved Son of God."

I have often been asked, If those phenomena are produced by our own spirits, how is it that we are ignorant of the fact? I reply, Man is only half known to himself. The man awake has no knowledge of the man asleep, nor the man asleep of the man awake. The somnambule has no knowledge of the normal man, nor the normal man of the somnambule. The chrysalis has no knowledge of the butterfly, nor the butterfly any remembrance of the chrysalis. We know that the ordinary man is ignorant of the entranced man, and the entranced man, on returning to soul life, has at once lost all knowledge and memory of the entranced man, who one minute before astonished us by his scientific knowledge. My diagram may help you to see *how* this is so. It shows the earth-plane and the spirit-plane as two states, separated by the wall or river of oblivion, and yet by habitual entrancements we learn to remember both spheres.

I desire, however, here to add that Christ, as "the Son of Man which is in heaven," dwelt daily both on earth and in heaven, and was for ever conscious of both lives, and thus He obtained power and applied titles to Himself presumptuous to mere man.

Of course my illustration, page 17, is only a diagram, but some forty years ago I had a curious corroboration of the idea of a door leading to the other life. At the time when Sir James Simpson introduced the use of chloroform as an anæsthetic, medical students amused themselves by experimenting with it on their own bodies. One day a friend of mine of Oriental blood, took chloroform, and described his sensations.

He said he felt himself whirling round and round in ever-diminishing circles, when at last he perceived a small round hole, through which he darted and became oblivious.

I believe the action of anæsthetics is to entrance the man. On one occasion, after taking chloroform for the relief of an intense pain, I distinctly found myself outside my body, as given in detail in my paper on anæsthetics.

True Spiritualism is the highest of all the sciences, because it reveals to us a knowledge of the world which now is, and of that which is to come, demonstrating that the spirit of man is supreme over, and independent of matter, and therefore immortal.

We are told by Christ that those who live the life shall know the doctrine, and the most ancient religions, philosophies, and mystics tell us the same thing. Man, they say, is a spiritual being, and should have, if in his right place, the control over matter,.

and they teach that to obtain this control over nature we must, in the first place, obtain a perfect control over ourselves. We must live a severely pure life, and by contemplation, fasting, and prayer, develop our spiritual powers. That many in olden and more recent times possessed these powers is the teaching of the Old Testament, and of the Christian saints.

In olden times, in the Middle Ages, and in our day, there have existed side by side the white and the black magic, just as in the Bible we have angels of light and of darkness, the works of the Lord and the works of the devil. Both possessed spiritual power over matter, but whereas those who practised white magic did so as a philosophy and religion, and as a means to good ends, those, on the other hand, who practised black magic, did so merely to obtain power over human beings for the gratification of their own diabolical selfishness.

Even with the best and greatest, the possession of those spiritual powers must subject the possessor to dangerous temptations, so much so that even of Christ we read that being led by the spirit into the wilderness, and after fasting forty days and forty nights, and no doubt with intense prayer to God His Father, obtaining divine and miraculous gifts, He was yet tempted of the devil, to magically convert stones into bread, to cast Himself from the pinnacle of the temple, and to aspire to the kingdoms of this earth. This may be regarded as showing the crucial turning point of Christ's life. But He made no hesitation, replying to the tempter, "Get thee behind me, Satan, for it is written, Thou shalt worship the Lord thy God, and Him only shalt thou serve."

A belief in the capabilities of man's spirit over matter is profoundly interesting, but how few could thus become spiritualised and exercise these gifts without danger; for even the angels kept not their first estate, but, as Milton says, by "ambition, that last infirmity of noble minds," fell.

In *The Spiritualist* of the 7th of December there is an interesting exposition of the views of the New York Theosophists, by Colonel Olcott, but I regret to find find him saying, "We Theosophists of the inner ring adhere to the Oriental religious philosophies, as better guides to happiness than the Christian theology."

I suppose Colonel Olcott must mean the corrupted interpretations of Christ's doctrines, not the teaching of Christ Himself, because no one can conceive of a higher religion and morality than that of Christ; for in Him there is placed before us a life and an example, by following which we shall reach the truest life which now is, and the highest which is to come.

As with the Mystics, so Christ teaches the severest self-discipline as necessary to man's own salvation, but

He as emphatically teaches that to love, and work and even die for others if need be, is our highest privilege.

Selfishness is not only shown to be the essence of all sin, but directly or indirectly the cause of almost all disease, both acute and chronic, and love and unselfishness are shown to be the great cure for sin and disease.

The entire unselfishness of Christ was the cause of His entire sinlessness, and the power by which He cured the bodies and souls of men was the power of unselfish love.

Thus "Christ crucified" became the sublimest philosophy. It signifies the crucifixion of our affections and lusts which war against the soul. It signifies the daily death of the body, necessary to the daily resurrection of the spirit, and "all who have this faith will purify themselves as Christ was pure"; and thus it is that "love to God and love to man" are the sum and substance of all the law and the prophets, the essence of all religion and of all morality.

All who beheld Stephen as he, the first Christian martyr, testified to the truth, "saw his face as it had been the face of an angel"; and Jesus Christ, "taking with Him (as three witnesses) Peter and James and John, went up into a mountain, and as He prayed the fashion of His face was changed, and shone as the sun, and His raiment became as light." And yet this Being, although possessed of all power, for our example submitted to death; and thus by the total abnegation of self, by the renunciation of the devil, by the crucifixion of those affections and lusts which war against the soul, became as Christ crucified, dead in the flesh but alive in the spirit. And He who spent His life in care and sorrow, and with the perfect foreknowledge of a fearfully cruel death, yet went about continually doing good, healing all manner of diseases, forgiving His enemies, casting out devils, opening the eyes of the physically and spiritually blind, raising the bodily and spiritually dead—first was transfigured, and ultimately, as "Enoch who walked with God," was carried up into the presence of "His Father and our Father, His God and our God."

Having at one and the same time been a dweller on this earth, and an inhabitant of heaven, He thus, "the well-beloved Son of God," and the perfect, divine, and miraculous Son of Man, becomes the Saviour of the world, not by His righteousness being *imputed* to us, as some say, but by our adopting His righteousness, "the way, the truth, and the life," for now and for evermore. Thus it is, I conceive, that the pure in heart shall see God, and thus it is that God in the centre and in the circumference is the key to man, and Christ, to earth and heaven, and to universal law.

V.—THE DIVINE AND MIRACULOUS MAN.*

THE central doctrine taught in this paper is that by His transfiguration on the Mount, Christ manifested Himself as the Spiritual, Heavenly, and Angelic man, and that this manifestation was typical of that which is within the possibility of those elect few, who, living truly the Divine life, can evoke in ecstatic prayer the hidden, Christ-like spiritual centre of the soul, and that this act has in many instances been demonstrated in the lives of the saints.

We are told that man was created in the image of God. If so, then the Spirit of Man and the Spirit of God are of one essence, and the Spirit of Man is thus the *Son of God*, while Jesus of Nazareth, when he became the Christ, was emphatically the *well-beloved Son of God*. Jesus, as the *Son of Man*, taught the so-called practical or exoteric doctrine of love to God and love to man as the sum and substance of all religion and all morality ; and Jesus, as the Christ, or *Son of God*, taught the esoteric or spiritual interpretation of this love to God and man. The simple doctrine of love to God and love to man is sufficient for the *ultimate* salvation of all those who sincerely

---

* Read at the British Association of Spiritualists, 3rd March, 1879, under the title, " Esoteric Christianity."

attempt to live the life; but the esoteric or spiritual doctrine teaches how man, while on this earth, may *fully* live the life, and thus at one and the same time be actually an inhabitant of earth and of heaven.

I desire it to be understood that I have no more doubt of the historic Jesus Christ than I have of the historic Plato, St. Paul, or St. Augustine; but, at the same time, I believe that the word *Christ*, as used by Bible and early Christian writers, and by the mystics, signifies also that divine and miraculous spiritual man which we may all, to some extent, possibly become, and which Jesus of Nazareth pre-eminently was.

It is believed by some that Jesus Christ revealed to His beloved disciples secrets regarding His nature and doctrine, which were not openly taught to the people; but, however that may be, we know that when Peter, in answer to the Master's question, "Whom say ye that I am?" replied, "Thou art the Christ, the Son of the living God." Jesus answered, "Blessed art thou, Simon Bar-Jona, for flesh and blood hath not revealed it unto thee, but My Father who is in heaven": and He charged His disciples that they should reveal unto no man that He was the Christ.

Again, when Jesus took Peter, and James, and John up into a high mountain, and was transfigured before them so that his face shone as the sun, and His garments became as light, so overwhelmingly splendid that Peter, James, and John fell on their faces to the earth, He again charged them that they should tell no man what they had seen till He had risen from the dead.

So also, in the first chapter of John's Gospel, the Logos, or word or wisdom of God, is used to signify the esoteric Christ in a mystical manner; and Origen, who lived at the end of the second and the beginning of the third century, says in his preface to John's Gospel: "To the literal-minded (or carnal) we teach the Gospel in the historic (or literal) way, preaching Jesus Christ and Him crucified, but to the proficients, fired with the love of Divine wisdom, we impart the Logos."

Thus it is the nature of man and the method of his salvation, body and soul, by the invocation of the Christ, or the hidden light and spiritual life, which St. John says are *within* every man, that is the subject of this paper.

It is maintained that the theory propounded is in strict accordance with the exoteric and esoteric teachings of Jesus of Nazareth, and St. John, and St. Paul, as recorded in the Gospels and Epistles, and these records, notwithstanding many verbal variations, are accepted as genuine records of the life and doctrines of the founder of the Christian religion.

The miraculous narrative is also accepted, it being understood that a miracle is not a direct interference by the Creator with the order of nature, but is the substitution of the spiritual or god-like force of the Divine Man for the secondary or lower forces in nature.

That the spiritual man is in possession of this force is taken for granted, as a fact known to whoever has truthfully and laboriously investigated the evidence ; hence a belief in the miracles of Christ is a natural consequence of this knowledge, and marvellous it is that many thoughtful " ministers of Christ " actually doubt or deny the necessity of this belief, as if it were possible there could be a Christ without miracles ; for Christ being " the Son of God with power," must, as a necessity of His nature, be a worker of miracles.

The esoteric idea of the Christ of the Gospels and the Epistles is that the term Christ signifies the spiritual head or inner secret light of every man ; and thus the salvation of man, soul and body, is not a mere phrase, but a transformation realised by this inner secret and hidden Christ, or light, or spirit coming to His temple, man's body, and living and ruling there.

The spiritual man being thus known and acknowledged now becomes the true master, and as the highest, is thus ruler over all lower forms of matter ; and not only so, but man being thus truly a son of God, is thus in heaven while on earth, even as "the Son of Man who *is* in heaven."

The spiritual man thus evoked is the image of God

re-discovered and constitutes man a son of God, *the divine and miraculous man*, the Christ-like man, the worker of miracles, the supreme lord over all forces and materials, the converter of water into wine, the giver of sight to the blind, hearing to the deaf, food to the hungry, health to the diseased, raising the dead, casting out devils, and thus demonstrating that the spiritual man is supreme over the laws of Nature and " solid " matter itself and capable of transforming this vile body into the glorified body, the transformed spiritual body with angelic and heavenly associates, as on the Mount.

In short, as God created man in His own image, so the Christ-born man, as a son of God, is supreme over all forms and forces lower than Himself, and over all disease and sin, and is thus saved body, soul, and spirit.

It is not meant to deny that many who pass through the ordeal of what is popularly called " conversion " are so far born again as to their outward lives and inward thoughts, and in so far are saved by the Christ ; but it is maintained that this form of salvation is a mere shadow of the substance, and that it is not the true and absolute salvation or regeneration of soul and body announced by Jesus Christ as " the way and the truth, and the life " here and hereafter, inasmuch as these converts are not entirely Christ-like or the possessors of miraculous powers. "If any man be in Christ (or in spirit) he is a new creature; all old things have passed away, and all things have become new." Those thus saved are "one with Christ, as He is one with the Father"; and while on earth they are in heaven, even as "the Son of Man *who is heaven.*"

Let us contemplate the life, teachings, works, transfiguration, crucifixion, death and resurrection of Jesus, the Christ of God, potentially and actually the Saviour of the world, morally, physically, and spiritually.

This miraculous and Divine Being, born of a woman, but moulded in some mystical sense by the influence of the Holy Spirit of the Father while within the mystery of woman's hidden nature, appeared on earth about two thousand years ago.

A few of His years, during the prime of human life, were spent in communion with God, "being about His Father's business." When about the age of thirty, having fasted forty days and forty nights, and overcome the devil, He from the mountain preached the Sermon on the Mount, a matchless epitome of all moral and spiritual perfection, and then immediately began to put His moral and spiritual precepts into action, *transmuting* spiritual truths into moral and physical facts by going about continually doing good, and curing all manner of diseases, and teaching that love to God and love to man were the sum and substance of all religion and all morality. He hated intensely all cruelty and all lying, but especially all hypocrisy and formalism and priestcraft. He opened the eyes of the blind; He caused the deaf to hear, the lame to walk, the leper to be cleansed, and the demoniac to be purified and in his right mind. He raised the dead to life, and was Himself, as an evidence of His spiritual nature, transfigured so that " His face shone as the sun and His raiment became as light." He taught the law of self-sacrifice, or the crucifixion of the flesh, as a pre-requisite to that spiritual regeneration which is eternal life. He Himself "despised and rejected of men," abhorred by formalists, hated by the priests, was persecuted, scourged, spit upon, and crucified as the result of His perfectly true, holy, and loving life.

To be fully possessed by the Divine power, beauty, majesty, and significance of this God-begotten man, we must devour, as it were, the story of His life, His words and acts, His afflictions and crucifixion, with the intense earnestness as of a new revelation, and in one unbroken effort.

If read thus the story comes out with a power, truth, beauty, majesty, and love which are overwhelming; and he who, whilst thus surveying the complete Christ—the manifestation of such love and holiness on His side, and such hideous wickedness on the part of man—is not torn with a tempest of grief and admiration, has not yet entered into the depths of the truest emotion.

This Jesus Christ declares Himself, and is declared by others, to be the only-begotten and well-beloved Son of God, and the only Way, and Truth, and Life by which we can go to our Father.

In order, if possible, to see how such claims can be true, how Christ, as the Spirit, can be the Saviour of man, body and soul, let us attempt to discover the nature and capabilities of man, and his destination. No more profoundly interesting questions can be asked, and nowhere can we find so profound a solution as in the teachings and life of Jesus Christ, Himself the all-wise and divine man.

Man, according to St. Paul, and a true psychology, is a trinity of body, soul, and spirit.

The visible earthly body is not the man, but only the mechanism used by the *soul*, which is the man. The visible body is said to be composed of certain atoms called matter; which matter is only a series of forms assumed by certain forces.

Force being the *substance* of matter, there is no such thing as "solid" matter, and no two "atoms of matter" are actually in contact.

Matter being only certain forms assumed by certain forces, can be dissolved and become invisible by the action of heat and other forces, including spiritual force; and can be re-formed by man, as a spiritual force, into its original, or any likeness desired by the spiritual force controlling the secondary forces.

Matter can thus be rendered as invisible as the soul and spirit of man now are.

Inhabiting the visible body is the soul or mental force of the man, and this is the man on this earth and in this world.

This soul wills, reasons, loves, hates, and moves its bodily machine according to its affections. It lives in a physical world, and accommodates itself to physical conditions. It marries and begets children; it digs the ground, and grows corn, and wine, and oil, and sheep, and oxen out of the ground. It moves the body to eat these and other forms of matter, in order that it may appropriate their forms and forces, and thus rebuild its ever decomposing body.

The soul does all this and many other things for about seventy years.

It clothes its body in garments of skin, or cotton, or wool, or silk, and lives in a hovel, a cottage, a mansion, or a palace, according to its powers of appropriation.

The man who is clothed in cotton and lives in a cottage, and "eats his bread by the sweat of his brow," is often despised by the man who has a gorgeous house and furniture, and who is "clothed in purple and fine linen, and fares sumptuously every day"; and yet our *earthly* life is but as a grain of sand on the sea-shore.

In about seventy years all this *formalism* comes to an end. The body first gets stiff, the eyes dim, the hearing dull, and the limbs unsteady; and ultimately the man is said to die!

But it is not so; the reality is not as the appearance; for even as no so-called matter can be annihilated, neither can any force.

Matter is changed in form and position, according to the direction of the internal force; but the internal force of man being his *reasoning* soul, remains a reasoning soul after the decay of his body, just as an electric force remains an electric force, although the jars, and tin-foil, and wire by which the electric force is held captive or directed, are broken and strewn on the floor.

The soul, thus being at the death of the body free to act on its own account, remains the living and reasoning soul of man, useful or mischievous, happy or miserable, according to the thoughts, words, or deeds done in the flesh.

This is the doctrine of Christ and of all religious teachers, and it is in conformity with the wholesome instincts of the vast majority of human beings. It is also in harmony with man's highest happiness, and therefore we pronounce it true.

Those who will not or cannot believe this doctrine, are *abnormal* human beings, the victims it may be, of their own modes of thought; or, it may be, so organically constituted as to be incapable of apprehending the spiritual nature of man—just as from an organic defect some are colour-blind, and cannot distinguish red from green.

But man is a trinity; and just as his bodily form is inhabited and animated by his soul-force, so his soul-force, being itself after the death of the body still in form as a man or woman, is on its departure from the body either a wandering, and it may be a visible soul or ghost, or it may be confined as a purgatorial creature, doomed for a certain time to purgation as by fire. Or it may be that the soul, while on earth, having lived a life of purity, love, and holiness, passes into paradise, and lives with the angels and "the spirits of the just made perfect."

If this result is gained, then that soul has found its spiritual head, or centre, or essence, the Christ within it, and has become truly a son of God.

Thus the man becomes a saved and angelic creature in heaven. But just as man, as Adam—who was made in the form of God, and was a true child of God—lost his immortal life *here*, so man, when he finds and regains the lost and hidden Christ within him, becomes an immortal and angelic being: the divine and miraculous man even while on this earth.

Even if the story of Adam be regarded as mythical, it none the less expresses the mystical truth that the true man is a son of God, a Christ-like, miracle-working man, "having dominion over the fowls of the air, the beasts of the field," and all subordinate creation.

Thus we can find an explanation of the words of the apostle: "If any man be in Christ (or in holy spirit), he is a new creature; old things are passed away, and all things have become new." Thus also are explained the words of Jesus when He says: "No man hath ascended up into heaven, but He who came down from heaven, even the Son of Man who is in heaven." Thus also can be understood Paul's words when he said: "I knew *a man in Christ*, how he was caught up into Paradise, and heard unspeakable words, which it is not *lawful* for a man to utter."

This is the hidden and esoteric doctrine taught by Jesus, "the secret of the Logos," as especially revealed by John, namely, The Gospel, The Good News, or the coming of the kingdom of heaven on this earth, as demonstrated by the abolition of sin, disease, devils, and mortality, before the face of Christ, the Divine and Miraculous Man.

It may be asked, as by Nicodemus, "How can these things be?" and it may be replied, "Art thou a teacher in Israel, and knowest not these things?"

Jesus says: "Repent and believe the *Gospel;*" that is, believe in the *good news* of the coming of the kingdom of heaven, and let your prayer to the Father be "Thy kingdom come on earth even as in heaven."

Some formal evangelical sects teach dogmatically that the Gospel is the belief that "the blood of Christ has been shed as a price for the sins of the world." So indeed it has; but the blood of Christ is the life of Christ, for "the blood is the life," and thus it is that Christ, by His life, and teachings, and self-sacrifice, and transfiguration, and death, and resurrection, if adopted by us, becomes "the way, the truth, and the life," whereby we are saved.

By this faith sin and disease disappeared before Him, and He thus became the Saviour of the body. and by this faith the soul is cleansed and then glorified. The Gospel, or good news, is thus no mere form of words, or sounding phrase, but the actual fact that the kingdom of heaven has come to all who believe, repent, and live the *complete* life of Christ.

The fruits of this salvation are "long-suffering, patience, love unfeigned, joy, peace," and its gifts are the powers of the Holy Spirit, the spiritual man, with his Christ-like power to "heal all manner of diseases, and to cast out all devils from Himself and others."

These are not words, but facts. The spiritual man has not only "the life which now is, but that which is to come"; the original form in which he was created is re-discovered; and being in the form of God, a divine man on *earth*, he is supreme master of himself, and therefore of the external phenomenal world, because to the Divine Man is given the power to create, re-dissolve, and re-create externals by the force of his spiritual alchemy.

"Where two of you shall agree as concerning anything you shall ask, it shall be done for them of My Father which is in heaven," and "Lo, I am with you alway, even to the end of the world."

If this promise of Christ is true, and if we have not the promised miraculous proof that Christ is with us, then we may be good moral followers of Jesus; but we are not saved *here*, soul and body, by the blood or life of Christ's mystical power over all secondary laws, and therefore over matter.

It may be replied that this cannot be the true meaning of Christ's words, because since the days of the apostles no such powers have been possessed by mortal man.

But it is replied, not so, for in no age of the world has "God left Himself without a witness," and to those who have been enlightened this statement is known to be true.

Pre-eminently to re-create this vile body into a new and glorious body, and thus to "glorify God with our souls and *bodies* which are His," has been practically accomplished in all ages of the world, and divine and miraculous men and women have never ceased from the face of the earth.

Moses was an illustration of this when descending from Mount Sinai, where he for forty days communed with God, his face shone so that the people dared not approach him; and thus also Stephen, the first Christian martyr, whose face the people saw "as it had been the face of an angel"; and like events have happened in modern times, and in all times. The lives of the saints, as in the instances of St. Ignatius, St. Teresa, and Savonarola, are an unanswerable evidence of this assertion, and the history of the Church of Christ affords a continuous succession of examples of holy men and women while in ecstatic prayer becoming, as St. Teresa expresses it, *married* mystically to the Divine Son, and thus *actually* becoming *one with God*, as Christ said He was one with God.

Those who ascended to this spiritual eminence became elevated from the ground, while their faces shone with an effulgence, and their chambers became filled with light—exact counterparts of the transfigured Christ.

This statement will not be received by the natural man, but it is not the less true, as those who have been initiated know.

Those who have watched the beauty of the sleeping child whose angel is beholding the face of God, or who have hung over the "rapture of repose" in the face of the good, whose spirit has just taken its last embrace on departing, may conceive of the beauty of those "born of the spirit," and with such it will not "seem a thing impossible" that God should raise the "dead soul" to the manifestation of the effulgent spirit, even on this earth.

If it be now asked, as in the days of Christ, "Are there few that be thus saved?" it may be replied, as by Christ, "Strive ye to enter in at the strait gate, for many will seek to enter in and shall not be able," "for many be called, but few chosen," and "strait is the gate that leadeth unto life, and few there be that find it."

If matter be merely a form assumed by certain forces, then each man's form is the form of his soul force; and if so, it can readily be understood that when the soul is purified by a life of holiness, and when "forsaking the husks which the swine do eat," it says, "I will arise and go to My Father," that the Christ or spirit "coming suddenly to its temple," the entire man becomes transformed into a resemblance of the transfigured Christ.

And as the spiritual man is "in the form of God," he becomes God-like in act, as well as thought. He becomes a worker of miracles; and being a forgiver of sin, or a healer of the diseased, he can transform into his own likeness the bodies of those who believe.

The souls of these men and women have found their Christ or Spiritual Light, and are at one with the Father.

As the humble chrysalis is by the transforming

power of the sun's heat converted into the glorious butterfly, so the careworn and travel-toiled Jesus, by the force of His spiritual prayer, was transfigured, "when His face shone as the sun and His raiment became as light," and Peter, and James, and John fell on their faces to the earth before Him.

Thus it is that the spiritual man not only commands his own body, but can transform all lower forms, and the miraculous becomes his natural condition.

As "God visits the sins of the father upon the children to the third generation," we can thus easily see why the spiritual regeneration of soul and body is a rare and exceptional event, and all but unattainable, except among the "few who are chosen."

But if the sins are visited to the third generation, so also are the virtues; and we can see how it may come to pass that if children were only begotten and reared in perfect love, those of the third generation might become actually sons of God.

To attain this end we might well afford to "sell all which we have and follow Christ"; and we can appreciate the wisdom of that man who bartered all that he had, and purchased the one field in which was hidden the sacred treasure.

For thousands of years this hidden light has been from time to time found and acted upon, and men and women who, having "crucified the flesh with its affections and lusts, which war against the soul," have lived the Christ-like life, and been gifted with the miraculous power of healing and prophecy.

The moral teachings and beneficent life of Jesus are sufficient for the great majority of human beings; but the esoteric teachings of Christ are revealed only to the few, and it is with the esoteric only that "the spirit maketh intercession with our spirits with groanings which cannot be uttered." The simple good ones of the earth have "the promise of the life *to come*," but those esoterically saved by the Christ within them coming to His temple are, while on earth, also in heaven, and are already "children of the resurrection."

Jesus taught the law of love, which, if followed, *leads* to the kingdom of heaven, and thus the young man who had kept this law from his youth was told that he was *not far* from the the kingdom of heaven, but although not far from it he was not within that kingdom.

The water, in his case, had not been converted into wine; the *moral* man was not the *divine* man; he was a lover, but not the bridegroom; he was not, in the miraculous sense, one with God as Christ and His chosen are.

To be "Christ-like," then, is the sum of the idea herein propounded.

This is a commonplace phrase, but those who use

it generally only realise half its signification. The meaning usually attached to it is that of one who lives a loving, peaceful, true, and religious life; who daily is a peacemaker, easily forgives his enemies, and doing daily all the good he can, makes continual self-sacrifices.

This indeed is much, and few there be who attain to it; but this is only the moral or exoteric side of Christ's life.

As we have already said, when, in answer to the Master, the disciple replied, " Thou art the Christ, the Son of the living God," Jesus replied, " Blessed art thou, Simon Bar-Jona, for flesh and blood hath not revealed it unto thee, but My Father, who is in heaven"; and He charged His disciples that they should reveal the secret to no man.

Again, when Jesus was transfigured, when " His face shone as the sun and His raiment as light," and Moses and Elias were with Him, being on the same plane of spirit or heaven, He again charged His disciples that they should tell no man until He was risen from the dead.

We repeat thus secretly was revealed the *secret* or esoteric life of Christ, " the secret of the Logos "; and thus Jesus, while on earth, was at the same time the Christ in heaven, " even the Son of Man *who is in* heaven," and thus one with the Father. To be Christ-like, therefore, is " to be one with Him [and

G

with God], as He was one with the Father." It is to be a divine and miraculous man on earth and in heaven at one and the same time while on this side the grave.

But we live in a physical world, ruled by physical laws, and while here the command is given to "increase and multiply and replenish the earth, and subdue it."

It is not, then, orderly that the whole human race should now be over-spiritualised on this earth, for were it so, there being then neither "marrying nor giving in marriage," the earth would become a desolation.

There must be always hewers of wood and drawers of water, and the supreme men must be few and far between.

Although, then, it has been given only in rare and exceptional cases, and as illustrations of the possibilities of man's nature to be truly Christ-like, yet we may all, more or less, be like Christ in the second degree, and this is practically what we must all strive after.

There is one grand law: "Thou shalt love the Lord thy God with all thy heart and soul and mind and strength; and thou shalt love thy neighbour as thyself." "This do, and thou shalt live," for this is the sum and substance of all religion and all morality.

The love of one's neighbour as one's self renders all

immorality impossible, for with this love we could not steal, nor bear false witness, nor envy or decry, nor slander, nor hate, nor kill, nor degrade any soul, but love and honour all men and all women.

We could pardon our enemies, and "pray for those who despitefully use us and persecute us," "returning blessing for cursing," "enduring all things, hoping all things, believing all things."

As aids to this life, we must live simply, purely, lovingly, prayerfully, and contentedly, rejoicing always in the Lord.

It is good at stated periods to partake of the bread and wine of the altar, but it is better always "to eat our food with gladness and singleness of heart, giving God thanks." Hence that grace before food which has degenerated into a mere form, and of which most men seem ashamed, should be a sincere prayer to God, so to "give us our daily bread," that this bread may be by the spirit transformed into the body and blood or life of Christ in us; and who shall place limits to the power of thankfulness, and love, and gratitude, thus to transform the food for soul and body?

In food thus taken the water may become converted into wine, and the loaves and fishes into miraculous nourishment, and we may become nourished as the "angels who excel in strength." The exhalations of the body may become as frankincense, and the "odour of sanctity" be a realised blessing.

Further, "cleanliness (in body, clothes, homes, food, and thoughts) is next to godliness," and our sleep should be as that which the beloved receive, a time of stillness, and holiness, and nearness to God, when "our old men shall see visions, and our young men shall dream dreams," and possibly when, as it is with children, our "angels may behold the face of our Father in heaven," as, supping with these angels, we return at morning tide to our renewed and invigorated selves.

This body, being thus cleansed, should not be injured or maligned by foolish, grotesque, vulgar, unwholesome, or indelicate externals, for how hideous that this soul and body, which are the Lord's, should be by man sold for houses or lands, or the upper seats in the synagogues, or to be called Rabbi; and by women for the vulgarity and indecency of dress, in place of being clothed with the humility of a meek and quiet spirit.

But "the flesh lusteth against the spirit and the spirit against the flesh," and "the carnal mind is enmity against God"; therefore, our whole life must be a constant desire and prayer to be kept from all evil, and led into all truth; to be enabled to love God, to forgive our enemies, and to look for the kingdom of heaven.

The essential centre of all true, internal, esoteric, and spiritual religion is one and the same. It is a seeking after God, "if haply we may find Him." It is a cry after the hidden God within us. It is the nirvana or God-ward rapture of *repose* and *knowledge* of the esoteric Brahman and Buddhist. It is the mystical participation of the body and blood, the life of Christ in the Eucharist; it is the longing desire of the soul and body after our inner Lord, the Lord of the temple, the Lord of heaven and earth. It is signified by the wisdom of the Book of Solomon, by the divine Sophia, with whom the soul of Jacob Bœhmen danced with divine delight, by the Logos of the Alexandrian Greeks, or the operative wisdom of God in the world, "the word" of St. John, "the mystery kept secret since the world began," "God manifest in the flesh," the Christ, the hidden "light of every man that cometh into the world," "the light shining in darkness and the darkness comprehending it not," "the bread of life which cometh down from heaven, and of which, if a man eat, he will hunger no more."

True religion thus interpreted renders all sectarianism an impossibility, for its one law is love—love to God and love to man—and its result must be ultimately to fill the earth with the glory of God, as the waters cover the channel of the sea.

When the whole earth was given over to wickedness, and the love of God, which is an *expanding* force, had been entirely driven out of the world, the natural and scientific consequence was a real or symbolical collapse of the earth, and its consequent submergence. Out of this catastrophe the earth had so far recovered, until at the time of the coming of Christ, wickedness had again become ascendant with its hideous cruelties and inconceivable moral putrescence. Then the Saviour of the earth, and of man, body and soul, appeared, and by His law of self-sacrifice and love, which has grown ever since, and has in these days of seeking after truth grown rapidly, the earth and man have been saved from a second cataclysm. And the expanding force of the love of God is destined thus to change this globe into " a new heaven and a new earth, wherein dwelleth righteousness," when, " by faith, mountains shall be removed, and rough places made plain," and when " none shall say ' Know the Lord, for all shall know Him from the least even to the greatest.' "

But as " Christ crucified was to the Jews a stumbling-block, and to the Greeks foolishness," so spiritual religion is to the Pharisee or formalist hateful, and to the materialist absurd ; because the formalist, or the carnal or material mind, is at enmity with that spiritual wisdom which can only be spiritually discerned.

The man of mere words or forms, whether the words are the empty shibboleth of the sectarian or the mere nomenclature of the scientist, cannot understand or know spiritual things.

THE DIVINE AND MIRACULOUS MAN. 87

If we offer the Esquimaux the fragrant fruits of the earth, he rejects them with disgust; but if we offer him a lump of reeking blubber, he will devour it with gratitude.

So, also, if we offer the dogmatic religionist, or the mere formalist, the simple " beauty of holiness " as the essence of religion, he will deny it, and, if he had the power, might, as of old, burn him who offers it, with his teachings, in the fire; but offer him an incomprehensible series of phrases, or offer him outward garments and ceremonials as true religion, and he will embrace you as a brother.

And so, again, if you can prove to the scientist any insignificant physiological fact extorted, it may be, by a cruel vivisection, he will extol you and enrol your name in the annals of a Royal Society. But offer to demonstrate to him that man is a trinity of body, soul, and spirit, and that his visible body is a mere machine used by his soul, and that, when in a trance, you may cut his body to pieces with the owner's entire indifference; and that the internal soul can see without visible eyes, and hear without visible ears, and handle without visible hands, and see and know equally the near and the far, the present, the past, and the future; attempt to demonstrate the truth of this to the materialist, and that religion is the highest science and philosophy, and proves that man's soul and spirit are supreme over all secondary laws, and over matter, and that the spiritual man being master of himself, is a supreme master over matter, and can thus, as a spiritual force, pass through matter, which is a mere form of secondary force, as heat passes through iron, or light passes through glass ; attempt to demonstrate such truths as these to the materialist and he may desire either to place you in a madhouse, or may hale you before the magistrate in the attempt to cast you into outer darkness with stripes and imprisonment.

True religion, nevertheless, is the highest of all the sciences and of all philosophies, for it not only gives a key to the mysteries of matter, but because the salvation of our bodies and souls can thereby be demonstrated to be *physiological and psychological facts*, and those who begin to live the life will begin to perceive that the doctrine is true, and those who fully live the life will *know* that it is true.

The fact that magical powers may be possessed by men of a low moral nature, and used for foolish or vile purposes is no objection to the fact of *the divine and miraculous man*, any more than the fact that the greatest mental genius is sometimes associated with the most degrading vice is an objection to mental genius.

Should, however, any man attain to the spiritual supremacy over matter, he is not only in a position of the greatest responsibility, but of imminent danger, unless he gives himself entirely to unselfishness ; and indeed " it were better for that man that a millstone were hanged about his neck, and he were cast into the depths of the sea," than that he should use these powers for any purpose antagonistic to the glory of God and the good of the human race, or to the coming of the *external* and *internal* kingdom of heaven, the salvation of the *bodies* and *souls* of men and women.

VI.—THE LIFE AND TEACHINGS OF JESUS CHRIST.

AS AN AUTO-BIOGRAPHY.

This paper forms the preface to my Life and Teaching of the Lord Jesus Christ, as a continuous narrative of the four gospels * and aims at giving that life and teaching as much as possible in the words of the gospels, without comment, and, therefore, I have ventured to give it, as above, the title of an autobiography, and I may here add that before publication I submitted this epitome of Christ's life to eight Theologians of the various schools in the Church, who accepted it with approval.

In the attempt, humbly, yet most earnestly, to contemplate critically the nature of this mysterious and Divine Being, it seems well to give the briefest epitome of the life, using as exclusively as possible the words of the Gospels and of Jesus Himself ; and as these words contain not only revealed, but hidden Divine wisdom, the reader should deeply ponder them.

The names Christ Jesus, Χριστος Ιησους, signify the Anointed Saviour ; and the "[1]Angel of the Lord" announced to Mary that Jesus should be born of her,

---

* H. Froude, Oxford University Press.   [1] L. I. 35.

as "Holy the Son of God"—mystically "the Logos[1] or Word or Wisdom of God, the True Light that lighteth every man coming into the world; who giveth to those who receive Him the right to become children of God : which Word became flesh and dwelt among us, as the glory of the only begotten of the Father, full of grace and truth."

"[2]And the child grew and waxed strong, and the grace of God was upon him, and he advanced in wisdom and in stature, and in favour with God and man; while at the age of twelve all who heard him disputing with the doctors in the temple, were amazed at his understanding."

This Divine Being began His public ministry [3]about the age of thirty, and continued it, as is supposed, for about three years.

Being [4]baptised by John, "As He came out of the water the heavens were opened to Him and a voice proclaimed, This is my beloved Son in whom I am well pleased."

Shortly after this, "[5]being full of the Holy Ghost, he was driven by the Spirit into the wilderness, to be tempted of the devil" to acts of magic, and especially tempted to make himself Master of "all the kingdoms of the earth, and the glory of them," which from His miraculous powers He could certainly have accom-

---

[1] J. 1. 1.—18. [2] L. 2. 40 [3] L. 3. 23. [4] M. 3. 16.
[5] K. 1. 12; M. 4. 1; L. 4. 1.

plished, and have thus realised the ardent expectations of the Jews : but His "[1]kingdom was not of this world," and He replied to the tempter " Get thee hence, Satan."

Having driven the money-changers out of the temple He afterwards preached "[2]Repent for the kingdom of heaven is at hand": and He taught the doctrine of [3]Regeneration, or the necessity of being from the natural reborn into the spiritual man; but said "[4]narrow is the gate and few be they who find it."

After that, having " [5]remained all night in prayer to God," He preached the "[6]Sermon on the Mount," an epitome of all moral and spiritual perfection : in holiness, humility, purity, love, forgiveness of enemies, faith, singleness of eye, and " seeking first the kingdom of God"; and enforcing the doctrine of self-denial, elsewhere described as "[7]taking up the cross daily " ; through which He, by total self-sacrifice even unto a fearful death, "[8]gave his life a ransom for many," and showed Himself to be " [9]the Way, the Truth, and the Life," whereby only the soul can be saved and brought to the Father"; having declared Himself to be "[10]The Bread of Life," "[11]The Light of the World," and "[12]The Christ the Son of the Living God."

---

[1] J. 18. 36.   [2] K. 1. 15.   [3] J. 3. 1.   [4] M. 7. 14.   [5] L 6.. 12.
[6] M. 5. 6-7. L. 6.   [7] L. 9. 23.   [8] M. 20. 28.   [9] J. 14. 6.
[10] J. 5. 21.   [11] J. 8. 12.   [12] M. 16. 15.

He throughout his teaching vehemently denounced all [1]Pharisaism, priestcraft, and hypocrisy, and in open violation of Pharisaism, "[2]being grieved with the hardening of their hearts," [3]wrought many of His miracles of healing on the Sabbath day, and thus the Pharisees "[4]became filled with madness," and ultimately compassed His physical destruction.

He especially taught that in love to God consisted the whole of religion, and in love to man the whole of morality, for He said "[5]On these two commandments hangeth the whole Law and the Prophets," and "there are none other commandments greater than these."

He for ever taught the Fatherhood of God as of One who loved all His children, [6]making His sun to rise on the evil and the good, and sending rain on the just and the unjust"; and He said "[7]For God so loved the world, that He gave his only begotten Son, that whosoever believeth on him, should have eternal life." "[8] And this is Life Eternal, that they should know Thee the only true God, and Him whom Thou has sent, Jesus Christ." For the Fatherhood of God implies the Sonship of Man, and hence the brotherhood of the human race, and The Christ exhibits God with man, and thus shows External Life.

[1] K. 7.   L. 11. 42; 13. 15.   M. 15. 12; 23.   [2] K. 3. 5.   [3] L. 6. 6.
L. 13. 14.   J. 5. 10. 14; 9.   [4] L. 6. 11.   [5] M. 22. 40.   [6] M. 5. 45.
[7] J. 3. 16.   [8] J. 17. 3.

He taught the mystic secret, that "[1] The kingdom of God is within you"; but "[2] Except ye become as little children, ye cannot enter that kingdom"; "[3] for the things of the Spirit are hidden from the wise and prudent but revealed unto babes."

He said that He Himself was "[4] The Son of Man which is in heaven," and this He illustrated by His [5] Transfiguration, when "His face shone as the sun, and His garments were white as light," as a type of all children of men, who when ultimately fully re-born of the Spirit, become sons and daughters of God: as has been shown by those saints who attained to that mystical perfection, to which are granted the gifts of healing, prophecy, and illumination.

He gave the Lord's prayer, and said, "when thou prayest enter into thy inner chamber and shut the door, and if My word abide with you, ask in My name and ye shall receive, seek and ye shall find, knock and it shall be opened unto you; for all things are possible to those who believe, and if ye have faith as a grain of mustard seed mountains shall be removed."

Miraculous works accompanied all His teaching, and He said "[6] The Father worketh hitherto and I work," and "[7] Believe Me for the very works' sake."

These miracles were not mere wonders, but were all beneficent or significant.

---
[1] L. 17. 21. [2] M. 18. 2. [3] M. 11. 25. [4] J. 3. 13. [5] K. 9. 2. M. 17. 2.
[6] J. 5. 17. [7] J. 5. 36. & 14 11.

He healed "[1] all manner of diseases"; He gave sight to the blind and hearing to the deaf; He caused the lame to walk and the lepers to become clean, and He cast out unclean spirits. He stilled the tempest, multiplied bread, and raised the dead to life, [2] and quickened whom He willed and "[3] as many as touched Him were made whole."

He thus showed Himself, not only as "[4] Lord of the Sabbath," but as Lord [5] by faith and prayer, over Man and Nature. [6] For as Man and Nature are, or rather were, only the reflection of the mind and will of God, or the objective thought of God, thus making the natural and the supernatural one, so Jesus as the Christ, or as THE Son of God, as "[7] God made manifest," could by will recreate or regenerate the souls and bodies of men, and thereby show that "[8] the Kingdom of God was at hand," and thus "[9] to the poor was this good news preached."

These acts were not contrary to Nature, but were super-Natural; namely, accentuations of Nature, or Nature fundamentally revealed; that is, they were the results of the operation of a force beyond those of the vital and physical or secondary laws, namely, the operation of the ultimate or primal spiritual law, as normal to the Divine and Miraculous Son of God,[10]

---

[1] M. 4. 23.   [2] J. 5. 21.   [3] K. 6. 5-6.   [4] K. 2. 28.   [5] M 21. 21-22. J. 14. 12; 16 15.   [6] Gen. 1. 3. Ps. 33. 6, 7, 9.   [7] J. 1. 14. [8] K. 1. 15.   [9] M. 11. 5.   [10] J. 1. 12.

with power—the whole esoteric doctrine of the Christ being, that the sons and daughters of men, as regenerate, should have the Christ or Word in them, as their vital force, and thus spiritually, that is miraculously, become Sons of God, and so become "[1] One with Him as He was one with the Father." For the Holy Spirit is One.

Therefore if we grant a divine Spirit, as the Creator of the external world and man, then this Creator, as Spirit, must be the fundamental cause or Sub-stance of Matter. For Creation, as a manifestation of power *plus* intelligence, is a universal miracle; and if Nature has progressed by the evolution of the lower to the higher forms, it must have done so, because there was a pre-existing, higher than itself; it being inconceivable that matter *per se* could rise beyond its own level; and hence evolution is only another expression for progress, according to intelligence, order, and will. And if man's spiritual nature be in the "[2] Image of God," then man, when " in the spirit," must have "[2] dominion over all lower creatures " and forces, and [3] Jesus the Christ as THE Son of God, the receiver of "[4] the Spirit without measure," must logically be Lord over all Matter; and therefore, to speak of " The Christ of God " without Miracles, is not only meaningless, but a contradiction in terms.

---

[1] J. 17. 21.   [2] Gen. 1. 26.   [3] M. 16. 16.   [4] J. 3. 34.

Very shortly before His death, Jesus "[1] stedfastly set His face to go to Jerusalem," knowing that insults, torture, and crucifixion awaited Him ; and a week before His death He [2] entered Jerusalem in triumph, amidst the cries of " Hosanna to the Son of David " ; and when bidden by the Pharisees to rebuke, what to them seemed blasphemy, He answered, " I tell you that if these shall hold their peace, the stones will cry out."

" As [3] He entered Jerusalem He wept over it," and predicted its destruction, and entering into the temple He for the second time [4] drove out the money-changers, saying, " My house shall be called a house of prayer for all nations, but ye have made it a den of thieves ; and the chief priests and the scribes heard it, and [seeing how their craft was at stake] sought how they might destroy Him."

[5] In the evening He kept the Passover with His disciples, and instituted " The Lord's Supper," saying, as He brake the Bread and gave the Cup, " This is My Body and this is My Blood of the New Covenant, which is shed for many for the remission of sins—this do in remembrance of Me."

Then as the last act of humility and love, He " washed the disciples' feet," and then passing into the Garden of Gethsemane, He endured the agony of

---

[1] L. 9. 51. [2] L. 19. 40. [3] L. 19. 41. [4] M. 21. 12. [5] L. 22. 15-21. M. 26. 20.

His Spiritual Passion, as He prayed, "[1]O My Father, if it be possible, let this cup pass from Me; and being in an agony He prayed more earnestly, His sweat being as great drops of blood falling to the ground."

Being then seized, He was condemned to death, and spat upon, and for mankind suffered the hideous tortures of Roman scourging and crucifixion, while He said, "Father, forgive them, for they know not what they do," and hanging on the Cross He cried with a loud voice, "My God, My God, why hast Thou forsaken Me?" and then, "Father, into Thy hands I commend My Spirit; and He bowed His head and gave up the ghost."

His body being wrapped in linen clothes, was laid in a tomb hewn out of the rock, and lay there for part of three days and nights, or about thirty-six hours; after which He rose from the dead, [2] while "the earth did quake and the veil of the temple was rent in twain from the top to the bottom," and thus especially showed His lordship over matter, as He broke down "the middle wall of partition," the veil between body and spirit, and visibly fulfilled His mystical words, "[3] I am the Resurrection and the Life."

During forty days He appeared at various intervals, [4] naturally and [5] supernaturally, to His disciples;

---

[1] M. 26.39. L. 22. 44.   [2] M. 27. 51.   [3] J. 11. 25.
[4] J. 20. 14; 21. 1.   [5] J. 20. 19.

and finally He blessed them, and "[1] while He blessed them He was parted from them and carried up into heaven"; having previously promised, "[2] where two or three are gathered together in My name, there am I in the midst of them"; and "[3] Lo, I am with you always, even unto the end of the world."

Thus Jesus of Nazareth, as the perfect Son of Man, the divine ideal Man, exemplified the law of human salvation, by a [4] perfect human life; and Jesus the Christ as THE Son of God—as the Logos, or Word, the Wisdom and [5] Glory of God, manifest in the flesh, "[6] The Mystery of God, even Christ in whom are hidden all the treasures of Wisdom and Knowledge," the Lord of Spirit and therefore of all forces, and over all Sub-stances, and to whom as a necessity of His nature, belonged all [7] power with "[8] legions of angels" if asked for—is the Saviour of the human race, soul and body, by His triumph over "the World, the Flesh, and the Devil," over Sin, Disease, and Death.

And thus, as the highest conceivable object of intellectual, moral, and spiritual perfection, as the manifestation of the essential as underlying the phenomenal, in Him, as THE Son of God, [9] we behold the Divine face, and comprehend how He is the ONE Central [10] Door, through which the entire

---

[1] L. 24. 51. [2] M. 18. 20. [3] M. 28. 20. [4] Heb. 2. 10. [5] J. 17. 5.
[6] Col. 2. 3. [7] J. 17. 2. M. 28. 18. [8] M. 26. 53. [9] J. 1. 18: 14. 9. [10] J. 10. 9.

human race must ultimately enter, and "[1]The flaming Sword" being quenched—regain its lost Paradise; [2] and "having overcome be permitted to eat of the tree of Life which is in the garden," and be thereby drawn back anew into the Heart of GOD.

---

[1] Gen. 3. 24.   [2] Rev. 2. 9.

VII.—MIRACLES

AS NOT CONTRARY TO NATURE, BUT AS DUE TO THE ACCENTUATION OF NATURAL FORCE THROUGH THE DIRECT ACTION OF SPIRITUAL POWER. *

IN all ages of the Christian Church, theologians, and in recent times, Butler, Mosley, Trench, and Westcott, have defined Miracles as Acts directly performed by the interference of the Creator, and as contrary to Nature, or as suspensions of the laws of Nature by the personal Act of God.

In answer to this definition, sceptics, and notably Hume, have said, " The Laws of Nature are fixed and invariable, and if so, then Miracles are impossible."

To this objection theologians have replied, " The Author of Nature could at His pleasure, alter or suspend the laws of Nature, and that, in the case of Jesus Christ and His immediate disciples He did so, as necessary evidences of Christ's Divine Mission, and

---

* This paper, in a brief form, appeared in the *Scots Magazine*, 1888, when I was urged to state my views in a more complete shape, and this I now attempt to do, and I may here say that this paper, when in proof, was submitted to the criticism of various thinkers and theologians.

that further, the testimony as to miracles of the witnesses present was complete and unanswerable."

To this the sceptics have said, "The teachings of Jesus are reasonable or unreasonable. If reasonable, they required no corroboration by acts contrary to Nature called Miracles ; and if unreasonable, miracles, even if they occurred, could not establish unreason ; and further, that at this distance of time it is impossible to confirm the evidence offered, and moreover, the confirmation of alleged acts, contrary to our universal experiences of natural laws, would require an amount of evidence infinitely transcending that required to prove any natural historic facts ; and lastly, that those who credit Miracles with the historic evidence of witnesses, are inconsistent with themselves, for they reject all evidence as to Miracles since the Apostolic Age."

The case for and against Miracles being thus stated, my position is as follows :

God is the author of Visible Nature. He is also the author of the Invisible Forces by the operation of which only Nature exists. For the creation of the universe must have been by an intelligence working by Spirit, through those forces which are now the sub-stance of matter.

The entire universe is thus the one universal Miracle, and hence, Miracles are not contrary to Nature, but are the essence of Nature.

The forces of Nature are, therefore, according to the Mind and Will of God, and are thus of infinite power and efficiency.

If so, then all acts occurring in Nature must be in accordance with the Mind and Will of God, as expressed in His Laws. And we therefore conclude that the invisible, as well as the visible universe, is only the reflection of the Divine Will. If so, then Miracles being acts in and on Nature, must be produced by the same forces which rule in the current order of Nature. Hence the natural and the supernatural are not contrary the one to the other, but can only be two degrees of One force; and thus I define Miracle, as *the result of an accentuation or modification of Natural force, through the direct action of Spiritual power.*

As illustrations of the accentuation of force on the natural plane, we find that radiant heat is produced by vibrations of the ether and light by a still higher accentuation or acceleration of these vibrations.

So also of the "Miracles of beauty" in flowers; the red colour is produced by certain vibrations, the yellow by accentuation of these vibrations, and the violet by a still further accentuation. And so also if we define certain diseases as the result of inefficient action, we can understand how these diseases could be cured by the accentuation of that action, as directed by Spiritual intelligence, thus working Miracles.

This is pre-eminently the age of experimental science, and we know as a sorrowful fact, that the majority of scientific men are Agnostics, having no belief in the supernatural or in Miracles. This scepticism more or less prevails everywhere, extending even to women in society, many of whom jauntily boast of their agnosticism and of their full sympathy with the Agnosticism of Science ; while some of the noblest of women have devoted their great genius in constructing deeply interesting works of fiction in support of their disbelief in the supernatural.

Further still, many broad church clergymen, if they do not deny the Miracles of Christ, gladly elude questioning on the subject and say to you in effect : " Even if the Miracles of Christ could be proved to be historic facts they would not affect our attitude, for we regard His life and teachings as divine evidences of His Moral and Spiritual perfection, of which no Miracles could increase our admiration and reverence."

To this I would reply that, although the Moral and Spiritual perfection of Christ's life and teaching may not require Miracles in attestation, yet this absolute perfection as existing in Christ only, out of all the countless millions who have appeared on this planet during, say six thousand years, is itself an evidence of the supernatural, and that such a being as the only fully begotten Son of God, must, like God, work

Miracles, from the power possessed by His Spiritual being over the the laws of matter.

Moreover, the Gospels, from the first to the last verses, are saturated with the idea of the supernatural, and it is only because the clerical sceptics assume that a Miracle is contrary to Nature, and therefore impossible, that they fail to see that the Christ without Miracles is meaningless and absurd.

The attitude of the scientific world towards Miracles was brought before me in a startling manner, when the volume of the *Encyclopædia Britannica* containing the letter M was published in 1888.

At that date I eagerly opened the volume to see and study the latest utterances of science on Miracles, and was much disappointed and surprised to find the word Miracle omitted. I thought that, as a universal dictionary, the word could not intentionally have been left out, and that at least a reason should be given why the subject was not discussed. Accordingly I wrote to the editor at Cambridge, but getting no reply, I again approached him through a personal friend of his, a distinguished professor; but even he got only a post-card in these words—" The subject of Miracles appears to be omitted by the plan of a work which excludes matters of dogmatic controversy." Surely an irrational excuse, when we find in the same work discussions on all other forms of religious and philosophic dogmas.

The question of Miracles would seem then to be excluded from the latest scientific dictionary, on the ground of the supernatural having no standing in what is called scientific culture.

This ignoring of the miraculous has no doubt arisen out of the wide prevalence of the doctrine of evolution, so profoundly fascinating to the scientific mind ; and here I desire to say that I sympathise with that doctrine, but I cannot conceive of any matter evolving from itself higher forms—unless there be a pre-existing mind, towards whose ideal, and by whose will, matter is caused to ascend, for matter, *per se*, cannot ascend above its own level.

Let us here ask ourselves what is science, and what is its fundamental position ? The answer is, that the object of science is to know the laws of Nature. But if the laws of Nature be only the expression of the Mind and Will of God, then the fundamental aim of true science must be to discover the Mind and Will of God.

In this light the pursuit of science is the highest possible occupation of the thinking and devout mind ; and instead of science and theology being opposed the one to the other, science is only another name for the highest theology, and thus true science and true theology are one.

If we apply this idea to the *modus operandi* of creation, we arrive at the conclusion that God created the visible universe of matter and the invisible universe of power, and that although "by the word of the Lord were the heavens made," yet the arm of the Lord which obeyed the word, was the force of Nature. It seems almost irreverent, if not profane, to say so, but it must have been so, for matter without force is non-existent, and the sub-stance of all matter is force ; and if we admit that this ultimate force in Nature, called attraction or cohesion, is of the nature of magnetism, then we arrive at the conclusion that the Divine Mind used magnetism in creating all things.

Sceptics have laid much stress on their objection to Miracles, because theologians have described them as acts produced personally by the Divine Mind, interfering with His own laws by suspension of these laws, and I cannot but sympathise with the sceptic in th objection, for such suspension would indicate a limitation to the Divine omnipotence of the Creator's plan in the universe.

Moreover, the theological idea does not seem to be corroborated by the historic facts, for, according to the records, we do not find that God personally interfered, but the record is that Miracles were always performed in the presence, and by the agency, of men chosen for the purpose, and Jesus says "No man hath seen God at any time ; the Only Begotten, who is in the bosom of the Father, He hath declared Him."

But man was made in God's image, and The Christ

was the entire image of God, and the fully regenerated are in Christ, and thus in God ; and so with these men, as with Christ, Miracles, as the result of the Will of the Spirit acting on those forces which are the substance of matter, were natural acts ; for Miracle is the natural act of the Spirit man, as ordinary acts are the natural work of the material organic man. And to deny this in the case of Christ Himself is, as I have said, not only meaningless, but a contradiction in terms.

Not that to be in Christ is essential to miraculous power, for we know from Biblical history and the history of all ages, that wicked men wrought Miracles, as said of Beelzebub—for Miracle is only this—the action of Spiritual beings on the force of Nature, and thus on matter.

Again there are those who question or deny the facts of Miracle, who yet believe that man is a Spiritual being, and as such survives the death of his body.

If so, then man, in the Spirit World, must be a continual worker of Miracles, for he must think, and communicate, and move, and act, on and in a world external to himself, and independently of an organisation visible to the eye of sense.

If so, then it becomes easy of comprehension, how this invisible spirit may, from time to time and under peculiar conditions, interfere in the affairs of man on this earth.

The history of the Bible is full of such instances, and Jesus Himself at His birth, His baptism, His temptation, His transfiguration, His agony in the garden, and at His resurrection, was helped by Angelic beings, and He repeatedly asserts that evil spirits contended with Him.

No orthodox theologian disputes these statements, but sceptics laugh all such to scorn, and speak of the belief in witchcraft as a mad craze of the days of darkness and ignorance.

But Moses, when he led the Children of Israel to the promised land, found witchcraft or devil-worship the religion of the people, and knowing that all such practices were entirely destructive of the souls and bodies of human beings, and led to the most horrible iniquities, he doomed all who thus practised, to extermination, as vermin in the land.

Sceptics, we say, have laughed all such statements to scorn, and yet the belief in witchcraft has come through all the ages even to this day, and has been believed in by the greatest minds in all times, from Moses and St. Paul downwards, and has not only always been practised among the Negro races, but at present, in the southern states of America, it is found to be on the increase among those liberated slaves who are left to their own devices, and many of whom, reverting to the habits of their race, practise all manner of devilries.

Witchcraft is only the association between the evil spirits of departed human beings and the souls of men and women living on the earth. It is obtained by the cultivation of all forms of vice and by what is called selling oneself to the devil, according to the story of Mephistopheles and Faust. Scientists, I say, may laugh at these statements as absurdities, but notwithstanding, the facts of witchcraft are known to many thousands of educated men and women now living.

But there is another phase of this subject, the investigation of which has long occupied the deep attention of millions of our fellow creatures, and that is the evidences as to the facts of modern Spiritualism.

This subject was taken up at the Church Congress, 1881, under the presidency of Dr. Lightfoot, Bishop of Durham; when the Rev. William Thornton and the Rev. Canon Wilberforce and others, while deploring the irregularities of Spiritualism, yet admitted that the facts were an unanswerable evidence against Materialism; and as Materialism is the religion which sceptical science wishes to set up, if Spiritualistic facts can refute Materialism, its uses for good must be immense; and it is very noteworthy, that the facts are believed in by our greatest living Naturalist, by our most subtle Chemist, by one of our greatest Mathematicians, and by our greatest poet since Shakespeare; while from the University of Cambridge has emanated a Society whose president is recognised as the highest moral and intellectual representative of that seat of learning, and whose work is, to separate the chaff from the wheat, and in the place of a speculative, to establish an experimental Psychology.

Descartes said: " I think ; therefore, I am," and of God we may say, " He thinks, and therefore all things are." If so, then the disembodied Spiritual man, by thought, as Swedenborg philosophically says, "surrounds himself with the forms of his affections." And just as with the natural man, whose imagination creates ideas, so with the Spiritual man, these ideas become objective facts, and as such beings say ; of *solidity;* beyond all human and terrestrial experience ; for here our surrounding world is atomic and phenomenal ; but the Spiritual world is unatomic and therefore insoluble and therefore eternal, whose centre is that Spiritual force by which all things are made; and thus we can understand the naturalness of Miracle to the Spiritual being. This, at least, is demonstrated, that Spiritual beings can move, dissolve, and recompose material sub-stances, and that according to their own assertions, they do so by controlling, without visible organisation, the forces of Nature as Spiritual alchymists.

If we apply these ideas to the natural man himself, we find this—when he lifts, let us say, a book from the table, he does so by his will operating on his brain, and his brain transmitting its message to the nerves and muscles of his arm and hand.

This is called a natural act, and yet the first impulse is from a Spiritual force operating *directly* on the brain ; and as we have defined Miracle as the direct action of Spirit through natural force on matter, this simple act of lifting the book is a Miracle, as wonderful and incomprehensible as any historic Miracle, the only difference being that it is performed through a visible organisation, while historic Miracles were performed through an invisible mechanism.

The facts of mesmerism go towards the establishing of the miraculous. These facts were long ridiculed by scientific men, but quite recently, under the name of hypnotism, the subject has become everywhere interesting.

These facts I have been familiar with for over fifty years, and I find that in the mesmeric trance, the Psychic sees, hears, and feels irrespective of the physical senses ; sometimes revealing hidden secrets, or describing acts occurring at a distance, or predicting future events ; while recently, in hypnotic cases habitual drunkenness and other vices have been immediately cured.

The Psychic in his entranced state, that is, when his Spiritual nature is evoked, makes promises of an amended life, and when he returns to his earthly body, although he may have no remembrance of the promise given in his Spiritual state, he yet religiously keeps to his promises.

Acts like these are analogous to those cases of sudden conversion which occur under the spiritualising influences of that ecstasy, which sometimes is the result of impassioned revival preaching, and in both instances they are a form of Miracle in the sense that a Miracle is the direct action of Spirit over matter.

In this connection I desire to draw attention to the evil practices of many French scientists now experimenting on hypnotic cases, in which suggestions are often forced on the Psychic, that at a said hour and day he or she may attempt to commit some crime.

This is a Satanic practice, and identical with the evil practices of black magic and witchcraft, wherein attempts are made to enslave the soul. The Spiritualistic explanation alone can account for these strange phenomena, and the practice of hypnotism and mesmerism should be in the hands only of those who are guided by truth, benevolence, and reverence.

With regard to the Saints it has been objected: that even if true, the Miracles of the Saints of modern times are feeble and even childish as compared with the one Miracle of the Universe.

To this I reply that, in this age of materialistic dogmatism, the fact that a grain of sand could be moved six inches by a psychical force, unknown to science, would be as significant as the stupendous revolutions of the stars in the appalling depths of infinite space.

But again it is urged, if evil Spirits, or idle or purgatorial Spirits, or magnetic influences, can work Miracles, the theologian will unite with the sceptic and ask—If Miracles can be produced from these inferior or evil sources, wherein lies the deep significance and solemn importance of the Miracles of Jesus Christ?

To this I would reply that, as Miracle is only the action of Spirit on matter, evil or wicked or foolish Spirits can thus act by reason of their nature; but when Jesus Christ came, He triumphed over all evil or unclean or foolish Spirits, who were leading the world to the infernals, and established the kingdom of truth and righteousnesss, by the brightness of His coming. He showed himself as supreme over all lower forces and over matter, and brought life and immortality to light. With Him all Miracles were significant or benevolent. With Him Miracles were as the efflorescence of the laws of Nature; they were as the heavens upbreaking through the earth—as the Voice of God moving on the waters, and were with Him the essence of His life.

This has been the voice of all those who became fully regenerated by the Spirit. Of those saints who by entire abnegation of self, became united to the Lord, and were enabled to say—being on the plane of Spirit—" We are one with Christ and one with

God." These Saints obtained "the perfect interior repose" and knew that—when in the Spirit, " To will in Christ was to create." To them were opened the secrets of the heart and to know as a fact that " the pure in heart shall see God," that to be single-eyed was to be full of light, and that to the eye of faith all mysteries become palpable realities. And to them was given the knowledge of the kingdom of heaven which is within us, with the gifts of healing, illumination and prophecy.

This claim is in harmony with the promises of Jesus when He said, "To faith all things are possible and greater works shall ye do than I do, and lo, I am with you always to the end of the world"; and surely in this age of all but universal scepticism, especially should the heart and soul now cry out for the living God, for an age which is for ever seeking self, and its own glorification, more than any other, demands the manifestation of miracles—*The Vis Medicatrix Christi.*

I recall the theory that matter is composed of atoms of infinite smallness, which never touch, but are in continual movement ; or that the ultimate atoms are only centres of force, and possessing polarity, and that such atoms can be arranged, separated, and rearranged, by chemical and magnetic actions as directed by the mind of man, as well as by the force of Nature. Then, if we conceive of man, as not only possessing mind, by which he by instruments manipulates the forces of Nature, but as being made in the image of God, and therefore possessing a spiritual nature, is it not easily conceivable that this God-like man should be able, like God, by *Will*, to direct the forces of Nature, so as to evoke a Spiritual chemistry, and thus call into existence from the surrounding elements, new forms?

If so, then let us attempt to apply these generalisations to the Miracles of Jesus Christ.

We read that Jesus went about continually doing good and healing all manner of diseases. We find also that the multitude so crowded around Him and so drew from His vitality, that, from time to time He withdrew into the mountains, and remained all night in prayer to God.

Those possessed by evil spirits, and the blind, and the lame, and lepers, came to Him everywhere, and He healed them all, and He quickened whom He willed, and as many as touched Him were made whole.

We may from these narratives conclude, that during His ministry many hundreds, if not thousands, of Miracles were wrought, but the cases specially given amount to only sixty, and these may be classified as follows :—

1. Miracles of healing and over demons.
2. Miracles in relation to animal and vegetable life and matter—such as the miraculous multiplication of

fishes; the blighting of the fig tree; water converted into wine; the swine driven mad.

3. Miracles over the elements—The stilling of the tempest.

4. Miracles connected with His own body—Walking on the sea; various disappearances and reappearances; the Transfiguration; the Resurrection and the Ascension.

The Miracles of healing present the fewest difficulties to the sceptic, because many diseases, which have resisted medicinal treatment for years, have been suddenly cured by mental emotions, and in recent times many diseases have been cured by simple faith or by prayer, and many are cured by change of habits or of air and food, while epilepsy has been cured by magnetic means, but no records exist as to the cure of congenital blindness or of malignant leprosy by such means.

These exceptional cases would require a creative Spiritual power over the tissues and the blood, beyond all experiences, in the power of mental faith, or prayer, or magnetic stimulants.

There further exists this distinction, that the healing power of Jesus was immediate, and infallible in its action.

But these Miracles of Jesus were not contrary to Nature, but might be regarded as accentuations of the powers of Nature by the direct Spiritual Will of Christ.

They were acts of creation, like those which originated the first ideas of the various organs of the body.

Evolutionists attempt to show how the organs of sense might be gradually evolved, but it seems inconceivable that Nature should create eyesight in animals unless the idea of vision was in the Divine mind. But granting this, then it is conceivable that the desire for sight might gradually, in unlimited time, become gratified, through the action of the inspired animal consciousness; and thus it becomes to me conceivable, *how* the Spiritual desire of Jesus might at once create vision. Granting this, all other instances of healing become easily acceptable.

If we take the case of blindness from cataract, it is conceivable that the cataract might gradually become absorbed by electric or other stimulation, and if the Spirit Mind can manipulate magnetic forces, as always asserted, it is easily comprehended *how* the Spirit Mind might at once cure cataract. Such cures being examples of the direct stimulation of natural forces by Spirit Will, and as such, Miracles are not contrary to natural action, but only differ in this, that natural cures are generally gradual, but the cures by Jesus were immediate, because in the Spirit plane time is non-existent.

I have already spoken of demons or disembodied human souls, as infesting human beings, and causing Epilepsy and Insanity. That insanity to a large extent is caused by demon possession, Jesus teaches, and modern experience confirms that teaching ; and that these demons can be exorcised and driven out, has always been the doctrine and practice of the Church, and also the doctrine and practice of mesmerists, and a belief in this is easy to the experimental Psychologist.

The Miracle of the swine being driven mad, and rushing down a steep place into the sea and being drowned, has recently excited the mirth of a distinguished naturalist : but this Miracle is as easy of belief to the practical Psychologist, as the belief in the cause and cure of human insanity, while the Miracle itself signified the destruction of all uncleanness.

The blasting of the fig tree might have been only the fulfilment of a prediction, the tree being withered suddenly, from some blight, and the signification of the Miracle being the destruction of pretentious hypocrisy. So, also, the tribute money found in the fish's mouth, might have been only an illustration of the faculty of pre-vision possessed by Jesus.

The conversion of water into wine, by an immediate re-arrangement of the component molecules of water, and its surrounding air, by the controlling power of a Spiritual alchemy, was a Miracle significant of the conversion of the lower animal man, into the regenerated Spiritual man, and might have been accomplished by the accentuation of a process analogous to catalytic fermentation. In any case the act was not much more wonderful or mysterious than the natural process of fermentation, itself an entire mystery, whereby the mild juice of the grape is converted into a spirit, which, if abused, brings ruin and destruction to whole races of men.

Moreover, the Miracle is one which it is claimed has been repeated by occult forces, and while on this point, it may not be overstraining the argument, to indicate the conceivability of the Eucharistic wine, in the presence of holy men, being in rare instances converted into a physical source of Spiritual life.

The multiplication of the loaves and fishes is probably regarded as the most inconceivable of all the Miracles of Christ, and yet it is not more wonderful than the fact that one grain of wheat might in one year, of three crops, be increased to one hundred million grains of wheat ; or the fact that one fish might, by natural generation, be converted into ten thousand millions of fishes in one year. One distinctive difference in Miracles from natural acts is, that the Miracle, occurring in the plane of Spirit, in which region there is no measure of time, occurs at once ; whereas natural acts require time, and yet the growth of magnificent flowers in Spring and Summer, from seeds so small as sometimes to require a magnifying glass for their observation, is as mysterious and wonderful as any Miracle.

There is, however, another possible interpretation of the multiplication of the loaves and fishes, that as Jesus was attended by Ministering Angels, these could have brought together this sudden accumulation of food.

The stilling of the tempest might, like the blasting of the fig tree, have been only a prediction; but if otherwise, I admit that I cannot apply the theory of the accentuation of Nature to its solution. But I doubt not that a Being who could control the forces of Nature as to the creation of tissues in the healing of congenital blindness, could control the forces which caused the wind and waves to arise.

The walking of Jesus on the sea admits of an easier solution in accordance with the laws of Nature.

We have all from time to time been conscious of sensations of dull heaviness at one time, and buoyant lightness at other times, and this may have arisen from our magnetic condition. It is admitted by men of science, that this planet may be in a negative magnetic state in relation to the sun, while man is said to be, in relation to the earth, in a positive magnetic state, and if so, then he naturally gravitates to the earth.

But in certain instances, well known to the students of practical psychology, this magnetic relationship has become modified during trance, and men have been then lifted from the earth. This fact has been within my own experience; while the Romish Church is full of like illustrations as to the levitation of the

Spiritualised Saints, and whether these Church instances be facts or theories, they indicate the naturalness, as it were, of the idea in relation to the Spiritualised man, and in this direction, we find no difficulty in comprehending how Our Lord, the Lord of all forces, not only walked on the sea, but ultimately ascended into the heavens.

But heaven was in Him, and He in it, and flesh and blood cannot inherit that kingdom ; and thus as He ascended, His natural frame ceased to exist ; and in this direction also, we find a solution of the sudden appearances and disappearances of Jesus, through the solvent power of Spirit over matter, as illustrated when the chains and bars ceased to exist as bonds, on the release of Peter from prison. For as we know that fire can dissolve and vapourise iron, so also we know that Spirit, as the creative power, can dissolve and re-create all the forms of matter according to its will ; this fact also being within the knowledge of the experimental Psychologist.

And so also in the Transfiguration, which signified the divine illumination of man, absolutely regenerated by the Holy Spirit—and as partially illustrated by the face of Stephen, the first Martyr, " whose face shone as the face of an Angel "—we are shown the transcendent " Light of the World " the Lord coming to His temple—the Son of Man shown to be in heaven, while on earth.

Lastly, we approach the crowning Miracle of Christ's life, the Resurrection of His body from the dead.

Jesus had said, " Destroy this temple and in three days I will raise it again " ; and also " I lay down My life that I may take it again ; and He said " I am the Resurrection and the Life."

In considering most reverently this crowning act of Christ's life, let us ask ourselves the question, What is Death ?

The answer is simply this, that death is the departure of the soul from the body. If so, then Jesus voluntarily submitted to an agonising death, as He cried with a loud voice, " Father, into Thy hands I commend My Spirit, and He bowed His Head and gave up the ghost."

After, as is supposed, about thirty-six hours, His Spirit returned, and entering His body, raised it to life.

This act is denounced by sceptics as one entirely incredible ; and yet we know that as an act, it is substantiated by other evidences.

Jesus had, during His ministry, illustrated the resurrection by three instances. He raised to life the widow's son, the daughter of Jairus, and Lazarus. The expression in the case of Jairus' daughter being, " Her Spirit returned and she arose and walked." If so, then we are justified in applying the same words in the other instance, and of Jesus we may say: His Spirit *returned* and He arose and came forth, as the watchmen quaked and became as dead men.

The Resurrection, therefore, as such, was not a unique act; but inasmuch as the Resurrection of Jesus was for a special purpose, predicted and effected by Jesus as His own act, it is a unique act in the history of the human race; an act whereby He triumphed over death and brought life and immortality to light.

The devout mind regards the Resurrection of Jesus as wholly ineffable and shrinks from applying to the solution of its mystery any ratiocination; and yet it must have happened by a process in harmony with the nature and relationship of soul and body, and if the Soul or Spirit of man be the real man, and his body only his earthly tenement, nothing can be more credible than that the Soul or Spirit may be able to leave its house and again return to that house. It was so with Paul, when caught up to the third heavens, where he saw things not lawful to utter, and it has been so with many saintly beings in the history of mankind.

In "The Christian Library," about the middle of the last century, as quoted by Dr. Crowell, it is recorded, that "The Rev. M. Tennant one day suddenly appeared to die, and being placed in a coffin was in due course about to be buried, but on the urgent solicitation of his physician, the funeral was put off for a time, and a few days afterwards the supposed dead man came to life."

On recovering, he affirmed that he had been in Paradise, and had seen that which eye had not seen nor ear heard, nor hath it entered into the heart of man to conceive ; and that the revelation was ineffable and could not be spoken.

Other instances of a like kind have occurred within my own experience, and it is well known, that those who have been drowned and afterwards brought to life by inflation of the lungs, have often declared that they have had visions of Paradise ; and similar experiences have often occurred to those who have experienced all the happiness of the blessed life, while their bodies were dead, while under the influence of chloroform, as they endured the horrors of fearful operations.

This line of reasoning is given in more detail in my paper on the Auto-noetic action of the mind, as a proof of the immortality of the Soul ; in which it is shown that to be in trance is to be dead in the flesh but alive in the Spirit.

Therefore, again, I would beg reverently to say, that although we regard the Nature of the Christ as ineffable, we are yet justified in believing that His physical Nature was in harmony with the laws of God as manifested in Nature, and if so, that His resurrection presents no insuperable difficulty to the human understanding.

Now, with regard to the Miracles of Christ generally, they were not mere wonders, but were all either benevolent or significant. He healed all manner of diseases; He gave sight to the blind and hearing to the deaf; He caused the lame to walk, and cleansed the leper and cast out unclean spirits, and raised the Spiritually and physically dead, and quickened whom He willed, and as many as touched Him were made whole. Thus in Jesus The Christ, as the highest conceivable object of Moral and Spiritual power, as the manifestation of the essential as underlying the phenomenal, we behold the Son of God with power, and One to whom Miracles were the essence of His Nature, and for the third time, I say, that the term The Christ of God, without Miracles, becomes not only meaningless, but a contradiction in terms.

It is quite true, as often objected, that the Spiritual significance of Christ's life and teaching is of higher signification than are the historic facts. But the Miracles of Christ have an infinite significance, for with Him, the curing of diseases and the forgiveness of sins were synonymous, while they demonstrated that the fundamental sub-stance of matter is Spirit, and that " all power belongeth unto God."

If so, then all the doubts and Agnosticism and Materialism and Atheism of this age of self-styled scientific culture, is only a passing phase, the result of surface knowledge, which is doomed, I fully believe, at no distant day to give place to that fundamental knowledge, with entire belief in *Science*, as nothing less than the Holy thing which is the Mind and Will of God, made manifest in the universe of Mind and Matter. In this light, to attempt to show that the Miracles of Jesus Christ admit of a scientific analysis, cannot be irreverent ; while, on the other hand, it may help towards a demonstration that the natural and the supernatural are not, as has heretofore been said, contrary the one to the other, but are only *two degrees* of the Will of God ; and that thus considered, revelation and true science are not opposed, but are only the deductive and inductive methods of Divine Reason.

VIII.—THE CHRISTIAN SAINTS;

THEIR METHOD AND THEIR POWER.*

IN my various writings I have repeatedly attempted to draw a comparison and a contrast between the method of the Oriental Mystics and the method followed by the Christian Saints.

In the address I delivered to the British Theosophical Society in January, 1880, I attempted to show that the powers claimed by the Oriental Mystics and the powers manifested by the Christian Saints were cognate, but that the method by which these powers were obtained, although *initially* the same—namely, the force of will or desire—yet immediately diverged or polarised in opposite directions.

The Oriental Adept, by soul or will force and a *systematic* training of his soul and body, attempts to seize on the Spirit, and thus to scale the heavens and there to rule as a demi-god.

The Christian Saint, on the other hand, undergoes no *systematic* training, but he ardently wills or desires to shun the world, the flesh, and the devil, and to "crucify those affections and lusts which war against the soul."

---

* Read before the British Theosophical Society, 31st July, 1881, and reprinted from the *Psychological Review*.

He takes Jesus Christ as his model, and attempts literally to realise the life and teachings of his Master. He believes that if he lives the life he will have a revelation of the doctrine, and he believes that if he knows the doctrine he will have a gift of the Spirit, and thus he desires to possess that knowledge which is Christ's power.

The Oriental Adept trusts to the powers of his own divine birth-right, the Christian Saint trusts entirely to the gift of God. The Adept asserts the power of his own will, the Saint desires with abject humility to submit to the will of God operating with his own spirit.

The pneumatological results are, sometimes, to a great extent identical; that is, both the Adept and the Saint become more or less spiritual beings with the powers of the Spirit. But the Adept, as he chiefly worships abstract power, lives in secret as a thinker and practical psychologist. The Saint, taking Jesus Christ in all respects as his model, expends his life in openly transmuting his spiritual powers into good works, and by his miraculous powers converting and regenerating the souls and bodies of the wicked and diseased men and women around him.

The Oriental Adept, by a long, severe, and systematic discipline, by pure diet, cleansings, and magnetic aid, attempts to regenerate his body.

The Saint has often committed the great error of

despising his body. He has abused it unnaturally and cruelly. He forgets that as his body should be the temple of the Holy Ghost, he should make it clean, strong, and beautiful. He disgraces his body instead of "presenting it a living sacrifice, holy, acceptable unto God, which is his *reasonable* service."

The Saint, in his attempt to imitate the sufferings of Jesus, seem to forget that these sufferings were of the soul, and thus it is that he often mistook the letter for the Spirit, and distorted the original into a caricature.

With reverence I conceive that Jesus of Nazareth, as Jesus, had a body of perfect health, and as the Christ had a body in all respects perfect, being a body regenerated as by water and the Spirit

The powers obtained by the Adept and the Saint are those of the Spirit.

They are what is called miraculous powers, by which I mean the central power of the One Spirit as distinguished from the circumferential powers of the complex soul.

By the central dynamics of the Spirit the possessor becomes a clairvoyant, a seer, a prophet. He can directly, or as an instrument, change the magnetic conditions, and thus rearrange the molecular constitution of matter, and thus heal disease, or ascend from the earth, or transmit his power and his form to a distance.

He can triumph over fire and water, subdue wild beasts, control madness, and convert the wicked into good men. As St. Catherine says, "Those in perfect obedience to God, receive the obedience of all creatures." But the Adept, so far as we know, is satisfied with the possession and *secret* exercise of these powers; while the Christian Saint, as an imitator of his Lord, openly expends his strength and his life in his desire to regenerate the souls and bodies of wicked and diseased human beings.

In my attempt to bring before the reader a true portrait of the Saints, I will give a brief outline of the lives of four Saints—two women and two men,—namely, St. Elizabeth of Hungary, St. Teresa of Spain, St. Francis of Assissi, and, lastly, the Curé D'Ars of France.

Of these four Saints, St. Elizabeth was a married woman; the other three were celibates. The three first lived in the middle ages, but the Curé D'Ars died only thirty-four years ago.

I shall attempt to show that these Saints, by the power of faith, love, purity, fasting, and prayer, obtained all and, so far as we know, more than Oriental Adepts obtain by physical and soul training and will force.

The Romish Church as a corporation, dealing as it does with millions of ignorant and superstitious men and women, chiefly of the Latin and Celtic races, has not unfrequently degraded the Saints in the eyes of thoughtful people, by showman-like, overlaying them with a childish garniture of tinsel.

Protestants on the other hand, in their blind intolerance of all that has arisen within the Romish Church, have not only remained deeply ignorant of the lives of the Saints, but have ignorantly laughed to scorn their asserted sanctity, and their miraculous powers.

But the Theosophist—knowing scientifically, as he does, the reality and power of the hidden spirit in man, and its godlike nature and attributes when evoked, and knowing the capability of man actually and potentially to become, as a matter of fact, a Christ-like being—can not only believe, but can truly and philosophically explain the nature and power of the Saint, his physiology and his psychology, the method and nature of his power—the *practical science* of the true Christian religion.

St. Elizabeth was a daughter of Andrias II., King of Hungary, and was born at Presburg in 1207.

At the age of fourteen she was married to the Landgraf of Thuringia. She had three children—a son and two daughters. Her husband died when on his way to Palestine when she was twenty years of age, and she died at the early age of twenty-four years.

As a Saint, her life has this peculiar interest, that

she was a married woman and had children; it being a general idea of Theosophists and others, that celibates only were capable of reaching the exaltation and marvellous powers of the supernatural spiritual life.

But although married, she was married to one who entirely appreciated her saintly virtues, and who was himself a perfectly pure and saintly man, living in simple love, and dying while on his way as a crusader to the Holy Land.

This St. Elizabeth, although a king's daughter, lived a life of what is called "the joy of holy poverty," that is, she gave up all worldly riches for the good of others, and received in exchange the graces, gifts, and powers of the Saint.

The power to heal disease, and to convert the wicked, and to work physical miracles, accompanied her during her husband's life, but especially after his death.

She worked incessantly among the poor, carrying to them alms and bread, while she herself fasted; and there is a well known picture which represents her as meeting her husband on the mountains, when on one of these missions, when the loaves in her apron were transformed into roses, symbolical of her beautiful and fragrant deeds, while above her head shone the luminous cross of divine love and life.

She not only gave all her property to the poor, but

nursed them in their illnesses, washing their sores, and associating with the terrible lepers.

Notwithstanding all which, being, after her husband's death, set aside by her brother-in-law, she fell into great troubles—was driven from place to place—resting in pig-styes, and was beaten, insulted, and slandered.

But, king's daughter though she was, she endured all this with the most beautiful patience, resignation, and love; esteeming herself only too happy to suffer thus the agonies of her Lord.

She had many beautiful visions of Christ, and experienced not only "the joy of self-sacrifice," but "the joy of *actual* union with Christ," or the *One* Spirit.

These early Saints, living in an age of darkness and cruelty, went to such extremes of self-abasement and mortification, as seem to me to dishonour God, as if their loving Father or their Lord, could possibly be gratified by excesses which were beneficial to no one, and which precipitated their own death. Mortifications which not only killed the body, but which were in themselves sometimes revolting and disgusting.

When in doubt as to the truthfulness of any action or mode of life, we cannot err in asking ourselves,—" Did Jesus Christ act thus, or did he teach thus?" and if He did not, then that action and mode of life is not in accordance with His will, but is an error, if not a sin.

But inasmuch as St. Elizabeth did all in faith and love, and errred because of the badness of the age in which she lived, her works may be said to have been counted to her as righteousness, and thus by the crucifixion of the flesh in love, she attained to the resurrection of the Spirit.

She believed all things were given to those who prayed in faith, and, while thus engaged, her face is described as becoming luminous, and her body as ascending in the air, as she saw and conversed with angelic beings.

After her death, it is said, her body emitted a perfume, her face became radiant, and the birds of the air sang her requiem.

Her utter unselfishness during life melted all hearts, and thus she received those spiritual and miraculous gifts which the *utter* surrender of the Self-hood to the Divine, seems, by the law of our higher nature, to secure.

St. Francis of Assissi, founder of the Franciscan order, was born *twenty-five* years before St. Elizabeth, in 1182, and died 1226, aged forty-four years.

It was from his influence that St. Elizabeth, in the first place, drew her inspiration.

He began life as a gay, generous, handsome, and extravagant young man, the admiration of his native city.

He was also a chivalrous soldier, but being taken prisoner, and falling into bad health, he came under spiritual influences, and from henceforth determined to live in severe literal exactness, according to the rule of the Sermon on the Mount and the Gospels

He adopted "holy purity and poverty," with their entire freedom from worldly cares, and having renounced all claim to his patrimony, he assumed the garb of the monk, and the avocation of the preaching mendicant.

He supported himself by begging from door to door, and lived on crusts of bread, and water.

His enthusiasm *necessarily* attracted many, and he and his associates became itinerant preachers of the Gospel, and boldly attacked all the vices and luxury of the age.

"He exalted poverty to an active and positive principle," for "blessed are the poor in spirit, and to the poor is the Gospel preached." Some of his followers became missionaries to foreign lands, and there denouncing what they considered idolatries, suffered martyrdom, and "their blood thus became the seed of the church."

Although his rule was severity itself, yet he himself ever remained the simple, humble, and loving man.

Like Daniel, by his purity, he subdued wild beasts, and he regarded all the lower animals as his brothers and sisters, addressing them in loving words, and the birds are said to have listened to him and to have obeyed his voice, ceasing to chatter when they disturbed his devotions, and ascending into the air singing at heaven's gate when he asked them to do so.

He wept as he saw lambs led to the slaughter, and the rivers and hills he also spoke to, as if they were his brothers and sisters.

Almost we might call him a Christian pantheist, for he believed that

> "He prayeth well who loveth well,
> Both man, and bird, and beast;
> He prayeth best who loveth best
> All things both great and small;
> For the dear God who loveth us,
> He made and loveth all."

He read the thoughts of men, and he cured their diseases, and frequently, in ecstatic prayer, visions of Christ stood before him, as he, rising in the air, became luminous, and the chapel was full of light, "For the eye being single, the whole body was full of light."

He wept much for his own sins and for the sins of others, and gloried in being despised and rejected of men.

His rule was purity, chastity, obedience, humility, love, faith, fasting, and prayer.

Finally, desiring ardently in all things to be worthy of the glory of carrying the cross of Christ, he became pierced with the Stigmata—the five wounds of the crucifixion.

These wounds he bore for two years. They were seen by many, although he carefully hid them, as too sacred for profane or curious eyes, and he carried them to his grave.

He was a man utterly devoted to his ideal Christ; by following whose rule literally and with intensity, he —being thus in the Spirit—by the creative power of imagination and love, became regenerated into the likeness of his Master, and with his Master's powers.

About 300 years later than St. Francis, was born St. Teresa, at Avila, in Old Castile, in the year 1515. She died 1583, aged 68 years.

From a child she was a mystic, and longed for martyrdom; and when 18 years of age she became a Carmelite nun.

She was, however, 40 years of age before the serious business of her life began in asceticism, and that continual desire of the soul—which is prayer—followed by visions and supernatural powers.

Unlike St. Elizabeth, St. Teresa was a woman of a subtle, metaphysical, analytical, and literary turn of mind, and for these reasons, and also because she lived in a more historic period, her life has for us a far greater interest than those of the older Saints.

Like St. Francis and others, she also when in ecstatic prayer frequently became luminous, and ascended from the earth; and she describes her spiritual visions as transcending all merely human imaginations, and altogether beyond human vision.

She describes some of these visions as that of the crucifixion of the flesh, which was as an *ecstatic pain*, and, in common with most of the Saints, being on the Spirit-plane, she encountered demons, and had conflicts with the Evil One.

A saying of hers was, "The highest power of the soul consisted not in thinking, but in loving"; and another saying was, "The highest perfection and power come from the total abnegation of self, and, by submitting our will to the will of others, we obtain the perfect mastery over selfishness and its sins."

In describing her ecstatic unions with Christ and God she uses the remarkable theosophic expression, afterwards used by Bœhme, " It seemed as if *the Spirit of my Soul* became *one* with God."

Thus also she obtained what in theosophic language she calls " *the perfect interior repose.*"

She also, with theosophic wisdom, says—"With God, to speak or think is to do or create."

Her revelations were more interior than external, and hence her physical miracles were fewer than with some other saints, but she still healed many sick folk.

She was beautiful in death, and from her body came the odour of sanctity.

With her was that clearness and exactness of reason which comes to the pure in heart; and she knew, as a biographer says, that " The *illumination* of the *understanding* was the *Science* of the Saints."

Her life is a deeply interesting mystical study; and Protestants without an understanding of such lives must continue to remain ignorant of those deep secrets of the soul and spirit which alone can reveal the *Hidden* Christ.

Lastly, I will bring before you the life of one—although not canonised, yet not the less a saint—Jean Marie Baptiste Viennay, commonly called the Curé D'Ars.

He was born at Dardilly, a village near Lyons, 1786, and died 1859, aged 73 years.

His parents were poor, simple farmers. He was always a simple and good child, and at an early age took seriously to religion.

He was a simple, pure, loving, and pious soul, and he set himself literally to live the life of Christ, like a little child.

Poverty, continual self-denials, the absence of all self-indulgence, total self-abnegation, humility, untiring forgiveness and charity, with continual prayer, were his rule of life.

He established an orphanage, himself occupying a humble chamber almost devoid of furniture.

He lived on crusts of bread and water; and if at any time kind souls, compassionating his poverty, left presents at his house, these he invariably and immediately gave away to the poor.

As one very *thinly* separated from the Spirit world, he encountered demons, and for twenty years was tormented by the Evil One, whom he called *Grappin*.

This demon came nightly to him for twenty years, calling out his name and denouncing him, knocking his furniture about, screaming and roaring like a condemned soul, and threatening his life.

These facts were substantiated by many sceptics who went for the purpose of testing their reality.

At first he was greatly alarmed, but he soon got accustomed to these things, enduring them with the utmost patience and good nature.

At last Grappin, finding himself despised, left him; but then began the persecutions of men—the neighbouring priests and others who envied his celebrity, or suffered from the reflections which his pure and holy life cast on themselves.

These persecutions included the vilest calumnies, but all this he not only bore with the sweetest patience, but rejoiced that he was found thus worthy to suffer for his Lord.

His simple goodness, charity, humility, and truth at last, after eight years, lived this persecution down; and some of those who had reviled him, came and on their knees and in tears asked his forgiveness.

Many miracles of healing were wrought through his

prayers, and the faith of the sick, especially cases of lameness and paralysis.

On one occasion, it is asserted, that with two or three pounds of flour, all that remained in the house, the housekeeper made about two hundred pounds of bread for the orphanage. She asserted that the batch rose and multiplied under her hands. Those who believe in spiritual powers and in the promises of Christ have no right to deny this statement.

On another occasion the granary was found empty, but in answer to prayer, next day it was found filled with corn.

The sceptic will at once say—" O, yes, by the hands of kind friends, who no doubt knew of the famine." But those who are acquainted with the phenomena of Spirit apports know that this asserted miracle might have happened.

He became and was, for twenty years, a centre, attracting pilgrims from all quarters; and it is asserted that from fifty to eighty thousand people were attracted to his remote village annually, that they might see him, or confess their sins, or be healed of their diseases of body and mind.

At these most laborious duties he, as a rule, worked eighteen hours a-day in the chapel for twenty years, without one holiday, an amount of labour on a minimum of rest and sleep and nourishment which seems supernatural.

He read the secrets of those who came for confession, and often told all before one word was confessed; and at other times if acts of sin were withheld by the penitent, he sometimes pointed out the day and hour such sins were committed.

At other times he could pick out of the waiting crowd those who stood most in need of his assistance, and many men of the world and sceptics were converted by a glance of the eye, a look or a word.

He prayed and wept much for his own sins and the sins of others; and on one occasion as he thus wept, the hardened sinner then under confession said: "Father, why do you weep so?" His reply was, "I weep dear friend, because you do not weep."

He was an unlettered man, but he also, like St. Teresa, had that clearness of mental vision and logic which comes to those whose eye being single their whole bodies are full of light.

On one occasion a man who earned a portion of his living by playing the fiddle at Sunday dances called on the Curé and begged for his prayers in aid of his crippled child.

The Curé, in confessing him, begged him to give up this fiddling. The man could not find in his heart to do so, but on returning home he suddenly repented, and breaking his fiddle into bits, threw them into the fire. As the wood burned the crippled child suddenly leaped from his bed, crying out, "I am cured, I am cured," as he ran through the house.

On another occasion the crippled child of a soldier was cured by a word; and another child, eight years old, believing in the promise of the good Curé, was "suddenly cured next day, and ran through the village like a hare."

He used to say many deep things, although himself so simple, as thus—

"A pure soul can get all it asks of God."

"When I give away everything to God he gives me all I ask."

"Prayer disengages the soul from matter—it unites us with God and fills us with light."

"It is Sin which brings all war, pestilence, disease, and death."

"God casts no man into hell: he casts himself there."

"The best way to be rich is to give everything, for then we have treasures in heaven."

"In self-surrender is the power of the saints."

"Those who are true and pure see all things with clear and exact minds."

He is described as one who seemed to be an embodied spirit before whose gaze and in whose presence all vanity and folly fled away.

His biographer says, "Faith was his only *Science* and explained all mysteries, while his intimate union with God showed all mysteries as *palpable realities.*"

A commentator says—"Sanctity is the fruit of Sacrifice: it is a death and a new brith; but there is no death without suffering, and no childbirth without its pangs."

Thus, the Curé D'Ars says, "When I could follow this rule I got all I asked, and fastings and vigils attract gifts from God."

Praise and flattery gave him positive pain, but under slanders and censures he felt peace and gratitude, saying, "how pleased he was that these good people had found him out."

He died as he had lived, in perfect peace, expressing only one regret—that his illness should give anyone trouble.

Thus passed away, in our own day, this sweet and beautiful soul—an illustration of the graces and powers given to those who fully live the entirely unselfish life, who, utterly emptying themselves of self, are filled with the Holy Spirit. Triumphing over "the world, the flesh, and the devil," in patience, humility, and love, they are regenerated as the well-beloved sons of God and brothers of Jesus Christ.

I have dwelt at greater length on the life of the Curé D'Ars because he lived in our own day, and thus not only touches us more nearly, but because his life and his words and his acts and his miraculous powers, have been witnessed by innumerable observers, many of whom are now living in our midst.

Those who believe in the phenomena of modern Spiritualism, can have no difficulty in believing in nearly all which is recorded of the Curé D'Ars and the other Saints described in this paper.

Those who may think it profanity to draw a parallel between the saintly powers of holy men and women and the many times disorderly and often wicked manifestations occurring among Spiritualists, or rather Spirit-ists, must remember that evil spirits can work miracles or wonders as well as good spirits; and it is admitted that modern Spiritualism, so called, too frequently no more resembles that spiritual power which comes through "holy purity" than the mischievous and unclean gambols of apes, resemble the dignified walk and conversation of good and high-souled men and women.*

It will have been noticed that many of the Saints, when engaged in ecstatic prayer, have been raised from the ground.

This is a statement which the sceptic will not readily accept, and yet the present writer knew a lady who, while on one occasion engaged before the altar, in intense prayer, began to find herself rising from the ground, but on becoming alarmed, re-alighted. Yes, there is a magic in intense prayer; and the elevation

---

* While admitting so much, I must still assert, that it is only through the *phenomena* of modern Spiritualism that materialism is refuted.

produced by Divine love is not only psychologically but physically true.*

The Saints were men and women, who resolved *literally* and *exactly* to live the life and follow the teachings of Jesus Christ, and thus they became born in His likeness.

By purity of life, by fastings, by self-denials, and by continual desire or prayer they became *spiritualised* human beings, and as such, according to the mystic teachings of Jacob Bœhme, they became Christ-like *actually*, and their will and imagination became creative.

Thus, "the Science of the Saints" is the Science of Theosophy and Christian Magic.

The mechanism of the saintly life is not taught by the Romish Church, but it would seem to teach that the Saints were so far mediums, inasmuch as their powers are often ascribed to the assistance of other departed saints.

Undoubtedly the Saints were mediums; but how far their powers were *centred* in their own spiritual nature, and how far they were assisted by angelic

---

* These elevations of the body, contrary to the law of gravity, occur only during ecstacy, and are mystically explained by the attractive power of Divine love, drawing the loving soul from earth to heaven.

Physically, I venture to give the explanation: that as two magnetic negatives repel each other, the earth being magnetically negative, repels that human being from its surface whose body is rendered magnetically negative by the total abnegation of selfishness.

beings, is difficult to determine. If any one be truly in spirit, or in the spirit plane, he is " in Christ " and at one with the Divine, and hence the marvellous powers thus manifested cannot be strictly individualised.

Jesus Christ worked miracles by His personal power, and yet even He was ministered to by angels.

Celibacy and extreme fastings are rules with the Saints; but this being a physical world, the great majority of men and women must marry, and increase, and multiply, and replenish the earth, and subdue it.

The entire Saint must therefore be an exceptional being, the singular spiritual phenomenon of his age, produced as a manifestation of the Son born of the Holy Spirit in the midst of a carnal world. "A light shining in darkness," although, as in the days of Jesus, "the darkness (for the most part) comprehendeth it not."

But although the entire Saint with miraculous powers must be an exceptional being, it is yet open to all to live a life of purity in body and soul—a life of self-denial in all things, including a simple diet, with occasional reasonable fasts—a life of humility, truth, charity, faith, and prayer, or continual desire for all good.

Those who can thus live, and especially if, in *patience*, they persevere therein, will at least so far become regenerated as to obtain an increase of health, beauty, happiness, clear mental vision, and magnetic healing power, and they will be able somewhat to comprehend *how* the Saints came to *know* that " Blessed are the pure in heart, for they shall see God."*

---

* In recent times various Societies have been formed for the investigation of Christo-Theosophy, but they have produced no results, because they have degenerated into mere debating societies, with discords; while a true Christo-Theosophic Society, I conceive, should aim at mutual encouragement in *the practice* of the Saintly life.

IX.—MESMERISM, HYPNOTISM, AND MIND HEALING.

IN this paper it is not necessary to go minutely into the history of Mesmerism, as the reader can find that in Dr. Gregory's book. But I may briefly say that to Mesmer, an Austrian physician, who flourished from about 1780 to 1815, we are indebted for the revival in our country of an occult art, known some 4,000 years ago to the Egyptian priests, as evidenced by many drawings on walls and mummy cases. That in London, about 1840, there was a Mesmeric Institution, of which Archbishop Whately was the president, and Dr. Elliotson the ruling spirit; and that for some ten years the subject, under the name of hypnotism, has been scientifically investigated with experiments at certain hospitals in France, Germany, and Holland.

The subject in Scotland occupied much attention about the year 1839, when Sir William Hamilton, Sir James Simpson, M.D., Dr. Robert Chambers, and Mr. Dove engaged themselves in many mesmeric experiments, and it was at that date that I first became acquainted with Clairvoyance.

The name hypnotism was first suggested by Mr. Braid, a surgeon practising in Manchester, who in

1843 published a book entitled *Hypnotism, or Nervous Sleep*.

Mr. Braid was convinced of the truth of the phenomena of mesmerism, but denied its leading theory, namely, that an aura proceeded from the operator to the patient, of a magnetic character. He asserted that there was no such aura, but that the phenomena of mesmerism were entirely subjective, and were mainly produced by a paralysis of the volitional power in man, and a substitution of the involuntary and automatic powers, and that, in effect, the phenomena were entirely due to the physical and mental condition of the patient, and independent of any agency proceeding from outside himself; and this is generally the theory now held by the Continental hypnotists, as described and illustrated by Dr. Tuckey, in his interesting book *Psycho-Therapeutics, or Curing by Suggestion.*

Now, in the first place, regarding this word hypnotism, we may say that it suggests no theory in solution of the problem in question, the word being simply derived from the Greek word for sleep, and we know that out of ordinary sleep no hypnotic phenomena arise.

But although the word itself suggests no theory, yet the theory attached to it to-day is, as I have said, the same as that given by Mr. Braid, and signifies the sleep of the volitional faculties and the awaking of the automatic conditions of the brain, which passively submits to the dictations and suggestions of the operator, and thus through the unconscious imagination, as it were, of the patient, suggests cures which in many cases are realised.

These cases of cure by suggestion, are illustrations of the power of the mind over the body—an extremely interesting subject, and one which is realised extensively in " The mind cure " of our day.

The question which I ask myself, however, in relation to this so-called cure by suggestion is this. How can the hypnotist explain why a suggestion given to the mind when in a *sleepy* condition should effect *permanent* cures, while the same suggestion given to the mind in its *rational* state fails to cure?

The hypnotist will say that the patient is in an inferior position while half or wholly asleep to the position he is in while in the full exercise of his reason, and yet grand curative results, both to body and mind, come through this inferior position.

I can understand how trifling or imaginary diseases may be thus cured, but I cannot understand how moral exaltations, as in the cure of confirmed drunkenness, and other degrading immoralities, can be thus *permanently* produced.

But the soul and body often are washed, as it were, and the unclean demons driven out, in hypnotic operation; and if so, I conclude that there is an efficient cause, and that the cause is not merely a suggestion given to the half unconscious mind of the patient, but must be the result of the inner and higher soul awaking out of its slumbers and assuming the command of the self-indulgent lower self.

If so, then hypnotism is only a means of producing trance, more or less complete, for trance must mean an awaking of the internal and hidden spirit, whereby the Spirit—The Lord—comes to His temple and drives from thence the concupiscences of the flesh; and here we have an analogy to certain cases of genuine and permanent and sudden "conversion of the soul" which sometimes result from the *entrancing* preaching of the words of righteousness.

If now we ask ourselves wherein does hypnotism differ from mesmerism, we must return to the question of the aura, said to be transmitted from the operator to his patient.

This aura is denied by hypnotists generally, but it is believed in by all mesmerists for the following reasons :—

1. When in good condition, but not otherwise, the mesmerist is often conscious of a certain tingling at the tips of his fingers, as he operates on the patient.

2. The patient without knowing of this, will sometimes say, I "feel a sensation coming from you"—it may be cool, cold, or warm, soothing or irritating, according to circumstances, and is sometimes felt to

be too strong, when the patient will request the operator to make the passes from a greater distance.

3. Sometimes in dark rooms the sensitive will say he sees the aura streaming from the hands.

4. This aura is on those occasions described as red, or purple, or violet, or yellow, or as in the aureola of the saint, white.

5. Patients can sometimes be magnetised through a wall or at a distance, they being ignorant of any such operation being attempted.

6. The aura has sometimes been rendered visible on the photographic plate.

7. The operator who cures, say a neuralgic pain, seems sometimes to cure vicariously, by the pain which he has cured in another, being transferred to himself, explainable by his having lost that aura which he has given to another.

The fact that Dr. Tuckey's book on Hypnotism passed through three editions in three years, is sufficient evidence of the hold the subject has acquired over the medical profession, who up to within some ten or twelve years, have always denounced mesmerism as quackery.

This sudden interest in Hypnotism, or Mesmerism under another name, would be surprising, were it not that it is only one more evidence that the thoughts of the few are interesting only to the few, because they are in advance of the age. But it for ever comes to pass that all things come to those who know how to wait; although the waiting is often long for the reception of new ideas, for if they in any way touch the *amour propre* of those in authority, they are resented for a period as offensive or dangerous, but afterwards, when the time comes, these ideas, under some new name or habiliments, are issued to an admiring world, as new and important discoveries; and so it is that while some men have laboured and laboured even unto death, other men with smiling and self-satisfied faces have, with much jubilation, entered into their labours.

Dr. Tuckey's book is called *Pyscho-Therapeutics*. But as the Psyche of Dr. Tuckey and of the French Hypnotist is a "function of the cortical substance of the brain," the term Psycho-Therapeutics seems to me rather misleading, for the Mesmerist and the Spiritualist do not regard the soul as a function of matter, but rather as the queen of the body; and, as the French views are entirely materialistic, one cannot understand why the Psyche should appear at all in their argument.

Further, the French theories on the *modus operandi* of cure by suggestion, which form the substance of French Hypnotism, are certainly, I should say, quite unintelligible to all but certain teachers of physiology.

For instance, we are told that the phenomena are to be explained on the theory of " The arrest of the function of a structure or organ by the action upon it of another function." This is called the doctrine of "Inhibition," and Dr. Tuckey says of it that "It offers an explanation of Hypnotic states, which is at least as satisfactory as that we have of the action of many drugs," and this valuation of the doctrine I would at once admit, because the fact is that the action of many medicinal substances in the cure of disease is quite inexplicable.

It seems to me that the hypnotic state is one more or less of *self*-entrancement, produced by fixing the mind on a *point*, and thus excluding all circumferential action. The mesmeric condition in entrancement is the same, and is likewise produced by the sensitive fixing his mind on the eye of the operator, as on a *point*; or it is produced by the *monotonous* manual action of the operator, paralysing, as it were, all circumferential mental action.

As an illustration: the Oriental fakirs produce *self*-entrancement by fixing their eyes on the tip of the nose or on the navel, the ears, at the same time, sometimes being closed by the thumbs.

The self-entranced soul may then act independently; while, on the other hand, the sensitives mesmerically entranced become the *mediums* for the will of the operator.

Both states are states of more or less entrancement, but what is entrancement?

Entrancement is a state in which the soul or mind or *ego* has more or less left the body—so that the body can be cut to pieces without experiencing pain; because the *ego* is outside, and is acting independently of the senses, as an autonoetic power, clairaudient and clairvoyant, and at times controlling its vacant body automatically.

But I would ask, how is the Hypnotist certain that by his passes he does not mesmerise his patients? Probably he often does; and this at least is the case, that he does not relieve them of their pains unless he first puts them into a state of hypnosis, and to attempt to explain this success by saying it arises from a state of *inhibition* or suspension of function, seems to me no rational explanation at all.

For instance, when a hypnotised subject promises in an unconscious state to abandon the use of alcohol, and when he awakes keeps his promise for weeks, or for years, it may be, and yet in total forgetfulness of any promise ever given, what theory of inhibition or suppressed higher function of the brain can explain this? Or when he promises to do some intricate and absurd action a week hence and at a given hour, how is the memory afterwards awakened by suppressed function, and this a week to a minute after the unconscious promise had been given? When questioned, the Materialistic Hypnotist can give no further explanation beyond a form of words, seemingly invented to hide his ignorance ; and yet we are told that Elliotson, Simpson, Gregory, Whateley, Hamilton, Chambers, and hundreds of wise men were in total ignorance of the subject " now scientifically explained for the first time."

I have given reasons for believing in the Mesmeric Aura, but I do not believe it is this aura which heals, but rather the will of the operator which directs this sympathetic aura.

"The blood is the life" of the body, and "good blood" may leave its transcendental manifestation in the aura which emanates from the sound hearted operator, who often in difficult cases of cure, finds himself as it were depleted, or as if he were laying down his life for his friend, a suggestion confirmed by the well known fact that it is unwholesome for a young child to sleep with an old nurse.

That it is the current directed by the will which heals, all mesmerists know by experience, for when their attention is not fixed on the case in hand, the result is for the patient a failure, and although the theory of an *Animal Magnetism* cannot be proved, yet the practical mesmerist finds it a theory which assists his efforts; and the mysterious attractions and repulsions which occasionally occur between two persons, without any discoverable reason, may perhaps have a psycho-magnetic origin.

I would briefly define hypnotism, as in ordinary

cases of cure, the submission of the soul of the patient to the will of the operator.

And I should briefly define mesmerism as an analogous operation, plus a psychical sympathy transferring a vital magnetism.

The hypnotist regards his patient somewhat as an automatic machine moved towards cure by suggestion, while the mesmerist rather regards him or her as a brother or sister in distress, to whom he desires to impart the blessing of sympathy.

In either case the power used is not only deeply interesting, but profoundly important—a power that may be turned to evil and malignant purposes, as in witchcraft, or that may be used in the love of truth and goodness.

If so, then the matter is not one for idle curiosity on the one hand, or for hard scientific exploration on the other hand, but should be regarded as a Divine gift, whereby, bearing each others' infirmities, we may fulfil the highest law.

It is dangerous for the uninstructed to amuse themselves with mesmeric experiments, but probably every healthy and kind-hearted man or woman could, by mesmerism, more or less relieve pain and cure disease, especially among the poor.

It has been proposed that mesmeric and hypnotic experiments and cures should be legally restricted to the medical faculty; but this I think would be a great mistake, for although itinerant mesmerists have often shown repulsive experiments, and sometimes damaged their subjects, yet, on the other hand, the view taken in the subject by medical men is almost entirely materialistic, while the experiments of the French schools have often been dangerous and degrading, and even criminal.

The poet is born and not made, so also is the true mesmerist born and not made by law or otherwise.

The good mesmerist does not require a minute knowledge of protoplasm or germ cells, but he must be a man of pure blood and kind heart, and sound mind, and he should believe in God and in man as a son of God. His desire must for ever be to relieve suffering and to confer happiness, and he must believe in the possibility of miracles of healing, in the sense that miracle is only the direct action of spirit on matter.

If so, then it would not be more absurd to assert that the only interpretation of the life and teachings of Jesus Christ should be exclusively in the hands of a dominant priesthood, that it would be absurd to teach that the law should give to legalised medical men an exclusive right to teach and practise the divine gift of magnetic healing.

Magnetic healing is a sacred subject, for it is the science of the power of mind and spirit over matter.

That this sacred science may be grossly abused in

the direction of devilry is most true ; but so also has liberty sometimes become synonymous with bloodshed, and so also has that religion, which should be of love, often become identified with hideous cruelties, but none the less are liberty, religion, and mesmerism, in safest keeping, when left to experience to define their truest levels.

Faith Healing and *Christian Science* may be regarded as cognate with mesmerism and with each other.

The "Peculiar People," taking St. James at his word, when sick did not send for the village doctor, but sent for the elders of their chapel, who came, and laying their hands on the sick and anointing them with oil, prayed that the Holy Spirit might raise them up and restore them to health and life as children of God. And when you reasoned with these good and simple people, and asked whether if they should break a leg they would still refuse to send for the surgeon, they were ready with the reply, that the children of God were as those of whom the Psalmist predicted, "A bone of them shall not be broken." These simple "Peculiar People" were ultimately represented at "Bethshan," or the Home of Rest, where ladies and gentlemen of holy lives and simple faith professed to cure all forms of disease by the simple rule of calling on the diseased to believe that on the laying on of hands the Holy Ghost must infallibly cure them, and it is quite well known that many were thus immediately and permanently cured of long-standing diseases.

The Christian scientists say:

1. Man is in his essence a spiritual being and a child of God.

2. If so, then as a spiritual being, man cannot suffer from physical disease.

3. If so, then the whole art of Faith and Christian Science Healing is, to deny that you are diseased, and to affirm that you, as a child of God, are in perfect health.

The teachers of this method will not assert that you are always at once made whole, but they teach that the persistent utterance of this faith must gradually restore you to health. That the mind has a marvellous influence over the body has always been taught by physicians, and it has been illustrated in those cases where "maternal marks" have been supposed to appear on the bodies of infants born into the world with skin marks corresponding to intensely-felt and sudden emotions of horror or disgust felt by the mother when pregnant; and if diseases can be thus produced by the mind, we may logically conclude that diseases may be likewise thus cured by the mind. A striking illustration of this power of imagination is recorded in the case of a criminal who was to suffer death by a slow process of blood-letting, and who being blindfolded, a trickling of water was arranged to flow over his arm, while those present commented on his gradual dissolution, the result ultimately being the death of the criminal.

There are also the perfectly well attested cases of the Stigmata, or five wounds of Christ, appearing on the hands and feet and chest of the Ascetic Saints as they prayed daily to suffer as their Lord suffered.

Again, it is a matter of common observation that the doctor who is sceptical of his powers effects few cures, compared with that doctor who by conviction, or by pretence, asserts that he can cure all cases coming under his hands. The real or assumed faith on the part of the physician is transferred to the patient, who is cured, not by the drugs which he swallows, but by the faith which makes him whole.

The great merit of the teaching of Faith Healing and Christian Science Healing consists in accumulating the evidences of the power of faith, and in the accepting as literal the saying of Jesus, " Whatsoever ye ask in faith that will ye receive "; and it must be immensely to the benefit of our sceptical age to encourage by all means this faith in God and in Christ and in ourselves as sons of God. But while this is so, it is not the less true that as we live in a physical world, we must attend to the laws of nature and obey their commandments. Paul says, " First that which is natural, and then that which is spiritual "; and in relation to health of body, the laws of hygiene are comprised in the word *purity*—pure air, pure water, pure food, pure bodies, and a pure mind. " Know ye not that your bodies are the temple of the Holy Spirit?" says the Apostle, and those who believe this purify themselves as Christ was pure.

It remains to ask the question, What are the limits of Faith Healing? We may freely grant that faith often becomes " the substance of things hoped for," and that the indulgence of hope and love transfigures the outward man, while in fear there is that torment which leads to despondency, disease, and death. In this light, under Faith Healing, many become amended in soul and body, but miracles do not occur except on the spiritual plane. The mere saying " I believe" will not cure inveterate or organic disease, but *actual* belief does. But that actual belief which does cure organic or inveterate disease is not attainable on the physical plane. It is the inheritance of the spirit, and hence entrancement has been found in mesmerism and hypnotism essential to the cure of deep-seated disease. No man, as Jesus says, by taking thought, " can add a cubit to his stature," and no man by simply ignoring that he is diseased can be cured of organic disease, although he may be, and often is, cured of functional diseases. By faith he rises out of those fears which are a torment, and which corrupt and degrade body and mind, and ascends into the pure atmosphere of "joy in believing," which brings renewed energy and strength. But so long as we live in a physical world it is absurd to deny that we can have diseased bodies, and it is not only absurd but it is wrong to deny these bodies. Our duty rather is to believe that these bodies can be rendered healthy and beautiful by the right conduct of the mind, and by faith in purity. If the doctrine be true that we have only to ignore our bodies in order to be filled by the spirit which heals, then we should, to be logical, ignore the necessity for food and ignore broken bones in a fractured leg, but the most ultra Christian Science Healer admits these exceptions.

By faith all things are possible. By mental faith most functional diseases can be cured, but the experiences of Mesmerism and Hypnotism show that it is only when in trance or when on the spirit plane that the deepest rooted diseases can be cured; and so far as I know, only one being has ever existed on this planet who, by a word, could at once cure "all manner of diseases."

But there is an attitude of the soul in prayer, whereby, shutting out all circumferential thoughts, one abstracts himself into the unity, and in this position it is open to anyone to ask relief from physical or mental suffering, and he or she will find that these prayers are often heard and answered, and that often immediately.

X.—CLAIRVOYANCE

AS A DEMONSTRATION OF THE IMMORTAL SOUL.

DR. GREGORY and other careful writers on clairvoyance have always distinguished between that form of clairvoyance called thought-reading, and that which may be called *direct* clairvoyance, or the power which the psychic has of seeing when blindfolded, independently of the knowledge of those present.

But although careful observers have made this distinction, yet I find that a large proportion of the cases published in various journals and books have not recognised this distinction, and, moreover, that the majority of cases thus recorded might come under the category of thought-reading.

All those therefore, who desire that mesmeric and other occult phenomena should be recorded not only with the most scrupulous attention to exactness, but with careful discrimination, must feel much indebted to *The Society for Psychical Research*, for their excellent reports on thought-reading, as recorded in their Proceedings.

The term clairvoyance is French, and means clear-seeing, but it appears to me to be an inadequate term, because it might signify clear optical vision, or clear mental vision, whereas what is signified by the term is the power which certain individuals possess, of seeing external objects under circumstances which render the sight of these objects impossible to physical optics. In short, by clairvoyance we mean the power which the *mind* has of seeing or knowing thoughts and physical conditions, and objects hidden from, or beyond the reach of the physical senses; and if the existence of this faculty can be established, we arrive at a demonstration that man has a power within his body as yet unrecognised by physical science—a power which is called soul or mind-seeing, and for the description of such a power the term might be autonoeticy (αυτονοητικος).*

Many cases of clairvoyance occur when the psychic is *apparently* in his or her normal condition—with the eyes open and the mind apparently normal. I say *apparently* normal, because I believe that in clairvoyance there is always an abnormal condition; but most cases of clairvoyance occur when the psychic is in a condition more or less of entrancement; by which is meant, a condition when the body can sometimes be cut, and the limbs amputated without any sensation of pain—a condition which might be expressed in the words of the Apostle, as being "dead in the flesh, but alive in the spirit."

I regard mind-reading as the most common form of clairvoyance, and the capability of seeing the contents

---

* Suggested to me by Professors Blackie and Donaldson.

of closed boxes or envelopes as the most rare form, because, as I believe, the faculty is generally connected more or less with the known, or, it may be, the unknown sympathy of human beings ; and hence the clairvoyant diagnosis of hidden disease is much more common than the seeing of inanimate objects inside inanimate envelopes or boxes.

There are almost innumerable cases of clairvoyance recorded in books and periodicals, and notably in Dr. Gregory's book on Mesmerism, and in the volumes of the *Zoist* and the *Spiritual Magazine*, but the instances I shall present for consideration have been gathered either from my own experience, or from the records of my personal friends. I have selected these in preference to cases from books ; partly because those which are published are open already for inspection, but chiefly because instances occurring within one's own experience, or that of personal friends, are brought before the mind with more detail and intensity, and are capable of more thorough investigation ; and in order to increase confidence, I have, where no objections were made, given names and addresses.

I first became acquainted with mesmerism and clairvoyance in Edinburgh in 1839, when my late friend, Mr. Dove, who subsequently became sub-editor of the *Builder* newspaper, was engaged in mesmeric experiments.

Mr. Dove was not only the most powerful mesmeriser I have ever seen, but he was also a man of extraordinary originality of mind, and his experiments and his philosophy founded on these experiments, excited much interest in the mind of George Combe, but especially in the mind of my friend, Robert Chambers, and in three distinguished men connected with the University of Edinburgh, namely, Sir William Hamilton, Bart., Professor of Logic (a believer in clairvoyance), Dr. Gregory, afterwards Professor of Chemistry, and Dr., afterwards Sir James Simpson, Bart., the celebrated originator of anæsthetics as used in the labours of child-bed. I mention Dr. Simpson because, notwithstanding some adverse remarks in his writings, he himself informed me in 1851 that he believed in the phenomena of mesmerism.

The name of Sir James Simpson is also introduced here because it is, I believe, in great part owing to the discovery and use of anæsthetics that mesmerism fell a good deal into neglect, as compared with the excitement created by the wonderful successes of Dr. Esdaile's Mesmeric Hospital in Calcutta in 1845; and indeed, I remember the celebrated surgeon, Mr. Liston, upon the discovery of the use of anæsthetics, congratulating his *confrères* that there would now be no further use for what he was pleased to call the mesmeric humbug.

Of late, however, the interest in mesmerism has

greatly revived, for one reason, because it is found to be intimately connected with Spiritualistic phenomena.

In attempting to analyse and classify cases of clairvoyance, they appear to me to arrange themselves in the following order:—

1. Thought-reading.
2. Brain reading of forgotten or absent thoughts.
3. Seeing bodily diseases, as if the body were transparent.
4. Psychometry, as described by Professor Denton, namely, the knowledge the psychic obtains by a *clue*, such as a lock of the hair of some absent person, or some portion of a distant object.
5. Seeing objects secreted in boxes or envelopes, or otherwise hidden or unknown to any one present.
6. Travelling clairvoyance, or seeing things at a distance beyond physical vision.
7. Seeing future events.
8. Entrancement and clairvoyance, as produced by the use of anæsthetics.

1. Thought-reading.—I have said that the facts recorded in the first paper on "Thought-reading," as drawn up by the Psychical Research Committee, present an overwhelming testimony to the existence of such a faculty, and when we find at page 27 of that report that the odds against the hypothesis of coinci-

dence in certain experiments as recorded, are upwards of 140 millions to 1, may we not say that the testimony amounts to a demonstration?

It is not necessary, therefore, that I should attempt to strengthen this testimony, but I may be permitted to give *one* additional illustration of thought-reading of a particularly interesting and illustrative character, as follows :—

A young lady, who has suffered much inconvenience as a thought-reader from her childhood, and who is intimately known to some of the members of the Psychical Society, having been lately called upon at a public institution to pass an examination in harmony, had a lesson set her on the black board, her own teacher being present. The solution of the problem was much beyond her ability, but her teacher, anxiously desiring that his pupil should succeed, but having no knowledge of her thought-reading powers, harmonised the passage in a complicated form in his own mind, when, much to his surprise, immediately the young lady took up the chalk and *note for note* wrote down on the black board the harmony as it existed in his own mind.

This, I think it will be admitted, is not only a striking, but a very interesting illustration of the faculty of thought-reading ; and, in estimating the force of this instance, it must be remembered that the mother, the teacher, and the pupil all assert that the exercise accomplished was much beyond the normal capabilities of the young lady. Does this case not suggest that successful pass examinations may sometimes in part be the result of brain-picking?

2. Brain-reading. — This differs from thought-reading in this, that the thought-reader desires you to think strongly of the subject to be read, but the brain-reader often not only reads the thoughts which are at the time absent from your mind, but he often reads thoughts which you have not only forgotten, but the existence of which you deny, until subsequently they are recalled to your remembrance.

Brain-reading is often met with when you experiment with sensitives, either in the dark or in the light, and on these occasions facts which have long been absent from your memory are often recalled by the sensitive.

In this place I may also mention that when you experiment with sensitives in absolute darkness, you may frequently obtain evidence of clairvoyance; for at your request any minute point on the hands or face will be immediately touched, and with the same rapidity and exactness as if you were in full light.

Further, with regard to darkness, it is well known to those who experiment with clairvoyants, that they are not so successful if the eye bandages are to some extent diaphanous as they are when the bandages produce absolute darkness.

This fact may perhaps not appear so incredible if we reflect, that when we attempt to think deeply, we often not only close the eyes, but we render the darkness greater by pressing the fingers against the eye-balls. While on this subject, I may observe that habitual clairvoyants become, it has appeared to me, liable to a deterioration of the eyesight beyond the average of human beings; but this is a subject requiring further observation.

As an instance of brain-reading, I may mention that on the 25th November I experimented with Mr. Hopcroft, and having entranced him, I presented him with twelve playing-cards enclosed in twelve envelopes, and asked if he could name the cards. This he entirely failed to do, but he at once said, "Those cards were not put into these envelopes by yourself—they were placed there by a lady; a tall, rather stout lady about fifty years of age. She has been in *Devonshire*, and you were not in the room when she placed them in the envelopes—you went out of the room in order that you might say you had no hand in it."

All this was exactly true, and there was no one in the room but myself and psychic. It was not thought-reading, for my thoughts were all in the direction that the sensitive should *name* the cards.

Four years ago Miss Tilly, of 36, St. Mary's Terrace, Paddington, was entranced in the presence of an epileptic, my desire being, if possible, to arrive at the brain or spinal cause of the disease ; but, instead of reading my thought, the clairvoyant said, "All I can see is that this illness has some connection with a horse," the fact being that the fits began after the lady had fallen with her horse in Rotten Row.

Some years ago I called on Mr. Wilson, 103, Caledonian Road, when he said, " This morning you had a giddy fit ; you also have a pain in your kidney, and you have a child ill in bed." He told me nothing else, and these three statements were perfectly correct. He could not possibly have known these things beforehand, and his information was not from Thought-reading, as my object in visiting him took my thoughts in a different direction.

3. Clairvoyance in Disease.—This is a most interesting faculty in itself ; but it has this further to recommend it, that its object is not mere curiosity, but the benevolent relief of human suffering.

Some years ago I had the good fortune to make the acquaintance of Mrs. D———. I told her I had a very dear friend who for years had suffered intense agony for hours every night in his back and chest, and that latterly he had been obliged to sit up all night in a chair, and that his legs had begun to swell.

Mrs. D—— expressed great sympathy for my friend, and most kindly begged I would let her see him, as she thought she would be able to suggest something for his relief.

This gentleman had regularly for three years been under many of the leading physicians of London. Some said that there must be some obscure heart affection. Others said it was neuralgia; one said it was gout; and the last consulted said it was malignant caries of the spine.

My friend met Mrs. D—— in my house, and she merely looked at him, and asked a few questions of an unimportant kind.

I then perceived that she wished to speak to me, and so I asked my friend to go into the next room, and when we were alone she said—

"I have seen what the disease is; I saw it as distinctly as if the body were transparent. There is a tumour behind the heart, about the size of a walnut; it is of a dirty colour, and it jumps and looks as if it would burst. Nothing can do him any good but entire rest."

I at once saw what she meant, and sat down and wrote to my friend's medical attendant as follows:—
"I believe I have discovered the nature of Mr. ——'s disease. He has an aneurism on the descending aorta, about the size of a walnut. It is this which causes the slight displacement which has been

observed in the heart, and the pressure of the tumour against the intercostal nerves is the cause of the agony in the back, and the peripheral pains in front of the chest. You are going to-morrow to see Sir James Paget in consultation; show him my diagnosis, and let me know what he says."

Next day the patient had this consultation, and at once Mrs. D——'s diagnosis was confirmed, and afterwards all the doctors who had during the last three years missed the true diagnosis now confirmed it. They also all agreed with Mrs. D—— that the only thing to be done was to take entire rest.

This treatment during years was more or less followed up, and with the result that the pains were reduced to a minimum.

But the disease remained, and six years afterwards the patient began to spit blood. Sir William Gull attended the case, and I occasionally met him, and one day asked him if he knew that I was the first medical man to suggest aneurism. He replied, "I know that, but I do not agree with you, for there is not one scientific sign of aneurism." To this I replied, "I know that it is aneurism." He replied, "I repeat, there is no scientific sign of aneurism." A few days after this discussion the patient died in a moment from the rupture of the aneurism.

4. *Psychometry.*—Dr. Buchanan, in 1849, found

that out of a class of 130 students at the Eclectic Medical College, Cincinnati, 43 signed a declaration, that if they took into their hands certain medical substances, concealed from them in paper, they suffered sensations and effects analogous to those experienced on swallowing those medicines—for instance, if they took Ipecacuanha, concealed in paper, into their hands, they suffered from nausea and sickness.

Reasoning and experimenting in the same direction, Professor Denton, geologist, Boston, wrote a book called "The Soul of Things," which has passed through several editions.

His theory is, that all bodies affect other bodies in juxtaposition, and that each infects the other, as it were, with its aura, or magnetism, or character, and that thus the geological rocks and fossils can, to the clairvoyant, reveal the history of the paleontology of the various strata. In illustration of this he gives a hundred clairvoyant descriptions of various fossils and bits of rock.

With reference to geological specimens, the experiments seem to me to prove nothing more than this, that the clairvoyants read Professor Denton's mind and confirmed his geological theories, and the fact that the specimens passed through his hands would alone be sufficient to infect or scent them, as it were, with his ideas.

I believe, however, that wearing apparel, rings, or hair belonging to an individual, can often act as a clue to the clairvoyant, and this is what Denton calls Psychometry.

I have two instances of this to offer you. For fifteen years I have worn a ring which my uncle wore for the last forty years of his life.

On one occasion, I placed this ring in Mr. Macgeary's hand, when instantly he was seized with spasm at the heart, and gasped for breath. My uncle had suffered from those symptoms, having died of advanced heart disease; but this Mr. Macgeary could not have known.

On another occasion, I placed this ring, which contains my grandfather's hair, in the hand of Madame Blavatsky, and asked her to describe my grandfather. She said he was a tall and slender man, with a red face; he took a good deal of port wine, and he had *blue* eyes. This was quite correct, but it was not mind-reading, as my thoughts were on my grandfather's character.

Professor Denton gives another instance. "A doctor was on the ice, and witnessed the death of a negro, who was accidentally dashed out of a swing against a block of ice and killed. The doctor went home, and began in the presence of some people to describe the accident, as he at the same time compounded and rolled in his fingers some pills. These pills were sent to an old lady, who had no knowledge of the accident to the negro, but she took the pills, and that night had a vivid dream of the catastrophe, in all its details, as if she saw it."

5. Clairvoyance in reference to objects secreted in boxes, or otherwise hidden from all present.

Mr. Hopcroft, to whom I have already alluded, was some time ago attending a séance at Mr. Younger's, Ledbury Road, when he said, "That lady," pointing to her, "has three and a half letters in her pocket." The lady replied, "That is a good guess, but I have only two and a half letters. I had another, but I took it out of my pocket just as I left home, and put it in my desk." Hopcroft replied, "That is strange, because I see three and a half letters in your pocket."

Nothing more was said about the letters, but just as the séance broke up, the lady exclaimed, "Well, you were right after all, for just as I left the house the postman gave me a letter, and I put it in my pocket and I forgot all about it."

This narrative is confirmed by Hopcroft and Mr. Younger, and by Miss Fearn, who were present.

The late Mr. Adolph Didier once narrated to me the following interesting cases, and I should say that I knew Mr. Didier for years, and I have always found him simple and truthful.

It has been often said by sceptics that there can be

little truth in clairvoyance, as no one has ever gained the reward offered for reading the number of a bank note enclosed in an envelope.

In reply to this statement, Mr. Didier asserted that on two occasions he read the numbers and gained the prizes.

Lord Ingestre once gave Didier an envelope containing, as he said, a £5 note, and said if he read the number he should have the note.

Didier replied, " I see only half a note." This was correct, and he received the reward.

On another occasion, at Bath, a clergyman offered him a £5 note if he would read the number, the note being enclosed in an envelope. He succeeded in giving the number, and he received the reward.

On another occasion, Lord Ingestre took a book at random from the shelves, and holding it closed behind his back, asked Didier to read the first four lines on page 27, and Didier succeeded in doing so.

On several occasions Didier, when perfectly blindfolded, played écarté with gentlemen who brought their own cards, and on these occasions he sometimes named the cards in his adversaries' hands, which, indeed, might be by mind-reading; but he also sometimes played his own hand without any one having looked at it, the cards lying as they were dealt, with their faces on the table.

In accordance with these statements, Captain James

tells me that he has seen Alexis Didier, brother to Adolph Didier, likewise play écarté with his hand lying on the table, face downwards, he being perfectly blindfolded.

I may add that the eyes of Didier in these experiments were generally closed by adhesive leather plasters, over which several handkerchiefs were tied.

Any sceptic may test the efficacy of leather plasters in producing absolute temporary blindness without the addition of any handkerchiefs.

Captain James also informs me that he has himself played Alexis Didier a game at billiards, his eyes being perfectly blindfolded; and Adolph informs me that he has also on various occasions, when perfectly blindfolded, played good games of billiards.

The following case is very instructive:—A gentleman placed in Didier's hand a closed envelope and asked him to read its contents. Didier took the gentleman's hand and said the words were *Can you polka?* The gentleman was delighted and relinquished Didier's hand, and said, "You are quite right."

Didier then placed the envelope to his forehead, and said, "No; I am wrong, the words are French—they are *Fleur de Marie.*"

The gentleman replied, "Oh no, you were quite right at first. *Can you polka* is correct." But Didier maintained that the words were *Fleur de Marie.*

The envelope was opened, and on the card was written "Fleur de Marie," much to the gentleman's surprise; but it afterwards transpired that the wife, in order to play a trick on her husband, had substituted her own for his writing.

This is a most instructive case, as it in the first place proved thought-reading, and in the second case it proved *direct* clairvoyance.

These cases were narrated to me by Didier himself, and they are also narrated in Didier's book on Mesmerism, published 1856, and dedicated to Lord Ingestre; but the case in which he saw "Can you polka," etc., is not recorded in his book as it is in this paper—the report in the book being that of a country newspaper, and, as Didier tells me, incorrect, but retained in the book as the evidence of a newspaper report of a public meeting.

With reference to clairvoyants reading unopened letters, the late Mr. Wedgwood, of Queen Anne Street, informed me that he was very intimate with a lady who had this faculty. On one occasion she read the contents of a letter before it had reached the house, and pointed out the letter among ten other letters presented to her by a friend; and the letter she selected, when opened, was found to contain the words she had seen beforehand.

The details of this case, as given by Mr. Wedgwood, are very minute.

Some years ago Mr. Redman brought his sensitive, Frederick Smith, a youth of 17, to my house, and experimented before myself, Mrs. Boole, and three other ladies.

He was blindfolded by means of soft paper folded double, and then gummed over his eyelids. This alone, as I and Mrs. Boole found, produced on us, when tested, so complete a blindness that we could not distinguish the brightly lighted gas globes. But in the case of Smith a silk handkerchief was tied over this paper.

Under these circumstances Smith took a pack of my own cards, and concealing their faces from all present—he being at one side of the table and we at the other—threw down on the table any card we asked for.

After this he read correctly on two occasions the first line on the pages indicated of a book we gave him—we being all ignorant of the words; and on another occasion he read a verse of poetry correctly, I merely pointing out the verse to be read, all present being ignorant of the words.

All present agreed that Smith was perfectly blindfolded, and that he proved himself to be a true direct clairvoyant.

6. Travelling Clairvoyance, or seeing objects at a distance impossible to human vision.

The late Mr. Rouse, on the 18th November, 1883, gave me the following narrative:—

When Mr. Gladstone disestablished the Irish Church, the title-deeds of a good many properties had to be examined; and among others the title-deeds of Sir Benson Maxwell of Donegal were demanded, but could not be found, and the advice of the lawyers was that the property should be placed in Chancery pending an arrangement.

Matters were in this position when a friend suggested that a clairvoyant might be consulted as to the lost deeds, but this suggestion was scouted by the family. However, the late Mrs. General Robertson, of 49, Victoria Street, taking a great interest in the case, on her own responsibility consulted Mr. Rouse. She sat with him at the table, and almost immediately Mr. Rouse was convulsively moved to take a pencil and a sheet of paper, and to write in large letters, "*Go to Exeter and make inquiries.*"

This message being sent to the family in Ireland, was by them regarded as absurd; but when Mrs. Robertson went back to Mr. Rouse, and sat at the table for further instructions, the same message, with increased energy, was given, "Go to Exeter and make enquiries."

At this stage of the case a friend in Ireland one day said to Sir Benson Maxwell, "Your father was very intimate with the Rev. Canon Boyd when he was in Ireland—why not talk the matter over with him?" Then it transpired that the Canon was then at Exeter, and Mr. Rouse's enigmatical instructions were called to mind. One of the family accordingly proceeded to Exeter, and had an interview with Mr. Boyd, who examined the contents of a large box in his attics, and found the lost deeds.

Mr. Rouse had no knowledge whatever either of the deeds or of Mr. Boyd's connection with them.

The details of this case are given in the *Spiritualist*, 7th April, 1876.

On the 20th November, 1882, I called on Mrs. Billing, who narrated to me as follows:—

"When I was at Chicago, I had a visit from Mr. Leonard Sweet, a distinguished lawyer, and a personal friend of the late President Lincoln, and it was told him through me that he had a certain package tied up with a peculiar cord in his safe at home. He said he had no knowledge of any such package, but he would look into the safe. He came back to me next day for a second sitting, when he was told that he had not kept his word, for he had not examined his safe, and he admitted he had not. He came back a third time, and said he had examined the contents of the safe, but there was no such package as described. He was told there *was* such a package, but it was inside a large envelope. He returned a fourth time, and said he had found the package in the safe."

Mrs. Billing also said—"Mr. Neville was engineer on board the *Jeannette*, American Arctic explorer. One day Mrs. Neville, being in New York, had an impression that her absent husband was near her, and she seemed to hear a voice say '*Listen!*' She did listen, and heard a ship's eight bells ring, and the voice said, 'We have just been crushed by the ice, but all are saved.'

"Months afterwards the survivors of the crew arrived at New York, and reported that the ship was sunk on that day, and at the hour of eight bells."

As Mrs. Billing gave me these narratives, Mrs. Magrae was sitting with her, and said, "Three years ago I was sitting with Mrs. Billing at 4, Keppel Street, when she said, '*Your nephew in Cincinnati is just dead,*' and twelve days afterwards the news arrived that my nephew had died on that day."

I can only add that I had known Mrs. Billing for years, and I had received ample proofs of her clairvoyant powers.

While on the subject of seeing distant localities, I may remark that there is a curious fact known to mesmerisers, namely this, the clairvoyants often describe localities as if they were reversed. For instance, they might describe a great club house in Pall Mall as on the north instead of on the south side of the street

Dr. Gregory mentions this, and adds it is unaccountable. But it has occurred to me that strong thinking may possibly project a picture of our thoughts as in a mirror, and hence the clairvoyant sees this image, as all pictures in mirrors are—reversed.

In the *Spectator*, 11th November, 1882, there is a review by the editor of the "Life of Professor De Morgan," by Mrs. De Morgan, in which the following case of clairvoyance is given. The Professor was dining in a house which Mrs. De Morgan had never seen. At this time she was engaged in mesmerising a girl for the cure of epilepsy, and the girl became entranced, and said—"I see the Professor; he is in the drawing-room, talking to the ladies and gentlemen;" and she also described the room and furniture, and said, "I see a tray with wine, and water, and biscuits." Mrs. De Morgan thought this must be a mistake, and urged that it must be coffee which she saw; but the girl would not give in, but insisted that it was wine, water, and biscuits.

Shortly afterwards the Professor returned home, and confirmed the girl's story in every particular as to the room and furniture, and the wine, water, and biscuits.

The reviewer says this is the best attested case of clairvoyance known, and he recommends it to the Psychical Research Society as a standard of credibility. It is certainly a good case, having reference to the unimpeachable veracity of Professor and Mrs. De Morgan; but there are many cases on record of equal importance, and attested by witnesses of equal reliability, and I think it will be admitted that my next three cases are as reliable, and perhaps more striking, than Professor De Morgan's case.

Mr. Podmore has sent me the following very interesting case received from Mrs. Ford, Adel Grange, Leeds. She writes—" In June, 1881, I sat with a clairvoyant in London, who knew nothing about me. He minutely described my house, and said, ' I enter the porch by *two* steps.' I replied, ' No, *one* step '; but he persisted there were two steps, and on my return home I found I was wrong and he was right. He also said, ' There is a little dog running about the hall, with long hair, which tumbles into its eyes.' I replied, ' We have no such dog '; but he persisted he saw it, and he described its colour ; and on my return home four days afterwards, the first thing I saw was this little dog, exactly as described, it having arrived with a visitor to the house during my absence."

There are some minute and curious details in Mrs. Ford's account, which space will not permit me to quote.

My late friend, Henry Thompson, Esq., of Fairfield, Yorkshire, a conspicuous figure in the mesmeric world some forty years ago, and an intimate friend of the author of " Zanoni," has sent me the two following excellent cases of clairvoyance. He says—

" On one occasion, being in the same room with

one of my mesmeric patients, who was asleep on the sofa, I rose from my seat and went to a box in the room in search of the copy of a will I wished to examine, when my patient said, 'You will not find what you want in that box; it is in a box under a window, at 3, Gray's Inn.'

"I had no idea it was there, but being in London a few days afterwards, I went to 3, Gray's Inn, and found the document in the box as described, in the office of Mr. Devrille." This case illustrates both thought-reading and direct clairvoyance.

Mr. Thompson describes his other case as follows:— "One day I was mesmerising Mrs. H., when she suddenly gave an exclamation and said, 'Your daughter has just fallen off her horse, and the horse is galloping across the park; but she is not hurt. She pulled herself off her horse when opening a gate, the horse having swerved, being frightened by a dog.'" Mr. Thompson adds—"This description was correct in every particular."

7. Clairvoyance as to future events.

This is the most difficult of all forms of clairvoyance to receive or to understand, and yet it is of much more frequent occurrence than reading words in closed envelopes or boxes; and spiritualistic literature contains many narratives in illustration of this faculty.

The theory is, that nothing happens by chance ; but all things follow a sequence of causes and effects, and that these can be seen and deciphered by some clairvoyants whose insight penetrates beyond " things which are visible."

My late friend, Mr. Joseph Hands, was an old surgeon, and lived at 84, The Grove, Hammersmith. He was one of the great Dr. Jenner's assistants, and in his book on " Will Ability," pp. 136-7, he gives an interesting account of how one of his clairvoyantes predicted that a certain patient who was dying of consumption would *not* die of that disease, but of stoppage in the bowels on the left side, and that he would die on a given day and at a fixed hour. This prediction was told to the sister of the invalid, but not to himself, and it all came to pass exactly as foretold.

Mr. Hands also narrates the following gipsy story, told him by Mrs. Francis, then residing at Blackheath :—

Before she was married she, from kindness, permitted a poor gipsy woman to pass through her confinement in a room over the laundry.

After the event was over the gipsy, feeling grateful for the lady's kindness, one day said she felt impelled to tell her of the future. She said, " You will be married clandestinely to a naval officer, and become the mother of three children ; but your husband will treat you badly, and forsake you, and afterwards die from an accident, and after a time the three children will all die within a few days of each other, and at last you will marry a second time."

All this happened exactly as predicted, and the lady, although protesting to the doctor that her first marriage was so unhappy that nothing would induce her to marry a second time, yet at last fell a victim to a barrister—the three children all having died of diphtheria.

On the 16th December, being on a visit to Sir Charles Isham, Bart., Northamptonshire, I met there Captain Norman Macleod of Macleod, who narrated to me the following cases, and kindly permitted me to use his name.

He said:—" Some years ago, being with my regiment at Gibraltar, I made the acquaintance of a lady clairvoyante, the wife of a brother officer.

"On one occasion the officers having arranged to have a horse-race, the lady being entranced, was in sport consulted as to the result. She replied, 'I see the race, the horses are now running, and I see the race is won by a black horse with white feet.'

"All present knew the horse alluded to, but laughed at the prediction as a good joke, the horse having, as we thought, no chance whatever.

"However, the race was duly run, and, to the astonishment of all concerned, the black horse with the white feet came in the winner."

On another occasion a gentleman connected with the garrison dreamt that a certain horse had just won a certain important race in England, and so impressed was this gentleman that he, when awake, got out of bed and wrote down the name of the horse so as to make no mistake.

Next day he told the officers of his dream, and the lists of all the horses were searched, but no horse bearing the name could be found.

There was no telegraphic communication between England and Gibraltar in these days, but about a week afterwards the news arrived that the race named had been won by a horse bearing the name the gentleman had seen in his dream.

This is an important case, as no guessing could have revealed the name of an unknown horse.

My friend Mr. M——, a retired surgeon, having in early life got into a circle of racing men, the day before the Derby, 1862, called on Mrs. R——, who said to him, " Mr. M——, do you believe in dreams?" to which he replied, "Yes"; "For," she said, " my friend Mr. S—— has three times dreamt that No. 17 on the card to-morrow will win the Derby."

Mr. M—— went to the Derby next day, and on the grand stand met Mr. J. J——, the leviathan bookmaker, and finding No. 17 on the card to be Caractacus, asked what odds were given on him, and Mr. J. J—— said 40 to one, and Mr. M—— laid £10 on the horse. Immediately another gentleman came up to Mr. J. J——, and getting the same odds, laid £25 on the horse. Mr. J. J—— said, "Won't you do it again?" "Yes." "Won't you do it a third time?" "Yes." And thus this second gentleman laid £75 on Caractacus

Immediately afterwards the Derby was run, and Caractacus came in the winner, and my friend Mr. M—— got £400, and the other gentleman got £3,000.

Immediately afterwards Mr. M—— heard a gentleman on the stand say, "A friend of mine has won a lot of money. At a spirit *séance* last night it was rapped out Caractacus was the horse, and he bet on him."

But this curious story does not end here, for Mrs. Crowe, a few days afterwards, wrote from Boulogne congratulating Mr. M—— on his success, and she added—" A *séance* was held here by some friends of mine three months ago, when two young Englishmen present said, ' If these spirits would tell a fellow what horse would win the Derby, they might be of some use'; whereupon the spirits rapped out, ' Caractacus will win the Derby.'"

Nor is this all, for as I narrated these occurrences to Mr. Rouse he said, " Well, that is curious. I never went to the Derby but once in my life, and it was the year Caractacus won. As I was looking about I met some outside betting men, and I asked what were the odds on the horses, and they gave me a card, and I spotted Caractacus at once, and a voice seemed to say that's the horse, and so I laid 10s. on him, and got 30 to 1."

With reference to clairvoyance being degraded by being turned into the selfish channels of betting and business speculations, Mrs. Billing told me the following story:—

A young gentleman went to a clairvoyante in New York, and begged she would give him some sittings for speculation, as he was just going to be married, and 5,000 dollars would be most useful in furnishing his house.

The clairvoyante replied that she never sat for such purposes; but he pressed her so hard that she consented to give him three sittings, and no more.

He sat three times and gained his 5,000 dollars; but not contented he returned a fourth time, and implored one more sitting. She reminded him of his promise to be content with three sittings; but he so urged it that she consented, but with a warning. The result was that he lost his 5,000 dollars.

8. Clairvoyance as produced by the use of Anæsthetics.—On this subject I will not here enter, as it forms a separate paper in this book.

In this paper I have recorded the details of forty

cases of clairvoyance occurring within my own experience, or that of my personal friends, and, if one may judge from the number of records (and I could easily have doubled them), which one investigator has met with, the amount of cases known to the community must be immense.

If one single instance of clairvoyance is demonstrated, it will prove that there is a faculty, or auto-noetic power in man as yet unrecognised by science ; and there can be only three ways of disposing of these records :—

1. That the narratives are all instances of falsehood or hallucination.
2. That they are merely cases of coincidence.
3. That they are records of facts.

But to those who know the sources of these narratives, the suggestion that they are instances of either falsehood or hallucination is absurd. The known veracity of the narrators excludes the first hypothesis, and there is no room for hallucination, in the fact that Mrs. De Morgan's clairvoyant saw water, wine, and biscuits in a room, or in Mr. Thompson's clairvoyant seeing a certain document in a certain box at 3, Gray's Inn ; or in Mrs. Ford's clairvoyant seeing and describing the little dog ; and no falsehood, hallucination, or coincidence could enable the brothers Didier, when perfectly blindfolded, to correctly play games of écarté, or games of billiards ; or enable Wilson to inform me correctly of the particular events which occurred to myself an hour previously, and three miles from his house.

I think one may be excused if he sometimes feels a little impatient with what appears to be *stolid* scepticism in these matters.

For instance, one sceptic, being forced by the evidence to admit the possibility of clairvoyance, said to me, "At least, let us be thankful so little of it is to be found."

Another sceptic, when a perfectly blindfolded clairvoyant read a sentence from a book, as held to his forehead, replied, "Well, it would have been more satisfactory if he had read with the back of his head."

But a third sceptic, when a clairvoyant read with the back of his head, said, "That act alone aroused my suspicion; for how do you know he did not place the page to the back of his head, in order that he might, by the aid of a small mirror concealed down his sleeve, catch a glimpse of the page!"

A fourth said, "Eyesight in the usual way was sufficient for him; and even if clairvoyance were true, he took no interest in it."

A fifth said, even if I showed him a case of what I called clairvoyance, he would simply say he was deceived.

But my sixth sceptic was the worst of all; for although he is popularly believed to be one of the greatest philosophers of the day, he yet, when I assured him I was as certain of my occult facts as I was of the existence of my right hand, replied, " I am not bound to admit the existence of your right hand, and as to your occult facts, if they were true, they would upset the laws of the universe."

In the face of objectors of this quality, may one not say—There are none so blind as those who won't see, and no credulity is so childish or so pedantic as some specimens of incredulity?

Doubtless, in matters of this kind, the evidence should be as exact as possible ; for, although verbal variations will not shake the belief of those who know that clairvoyance is true, they yet afford excuses for the disbelief of those who assert that clairvoyance is impossible.

For myself, I may be permitted to say that I believe the statements I have made in this paper demonstrate that there is a faculty in man of clairvoyance ; a faculty which might be called Autonoetic, or mind-knowing, independently of the physical senses.

As to the *modus operandi*, a clairvoyante, when in trance, said to me, " Electricity is the arm of God " ; and Bovee Dods says, " Mind can only touch matter through electricity." It may be that in clairvoyance mind employs an electric telegraph, using as its afferent and efferent wires magnetic lines of will force, analogous to the line of light in the photophone.

Many years of observation of these matters have convinced me that there is such a faculty—of this I have no more doubt than I have of ordinary vision.

The faculty of clairvoyance is comparatively rare, and is so far extraordinary, but to my mind it is not more wonderful than is the faculty of ordinary vision.

If one single instance of direct clairvoyance can be demonstrated, then one thousand failures to produce a second instance would in no degree invalidate the integrity of the first instance, and yet one continually meets with those who, having perhaps devoted a few hours to the investigation of this difficult subject, and failed to obtain a uniform series of results, denounce as dupes and simpletons believers, who may have given twenty, or thirty, or forty years to the investigation.

I can foresee that thought-reading, as the most common form of clairvoyance, inasmuch as the physical theory of sympathetic brain vibrations may seem to afford a materialistic clue to its solution, is destined at no distant day to be widely accepted by the scientific world. But this explanation does not satisfy my mind, and I believe further experiments will prove that all thought-readers are more or less psychics.

But in any case sympathetic brain vibrations cannot explain that form of clairvoyance which sees distant objects, through it may be miles of streets, or it may be through a segment of the earth's crust ; nor can sympathetic vibrations account for the revelation of secrets unknown to anyone present. Nor can brain vibrations explain how Mrs. De Morgan's maid persisted in seeing *wine, water, and biscuits* in a distant room, when all the vibrations of Mrs. De Morgan's brain desired that the psychic should there see *coffee* !

Somnambulism has always been recognised as a fact by the medical profession, namely, the faculty manifested in an abnormal condition of sleep, of accomplishing feats of physical and mental ability far beyond the normal powers of the individual.

In Chambers's *Encyclopædia* the Archbishop of Bordeaux narrates how a student rose from his bed in sleep and composed and wrote down a sermon, and wrote out music, and corrected it, and continued to do all this although a sheet of pasteboard was interposed between the face of the sleeper and the paper on which he was writing.

This was spontaneous clairvoyance, and if so, why should there be so much difficulty in admitting the facts of mesmerically-induced clairvoyance?

Psychology, as it now exists, is, as the word literally implies, a mere *talking* about the soul and its powers; but if Psychologists were intimate with the phenomena of clairvoyance, they would then be able to construct a *science* of the soul as founded on psychical facts.

I have said that clairvoyance is more extraordinary, but that it is not more wonderful than ordinary vision. The eye itself is an inscrutable mystery, for how rays of light impinging on the infinitesimal terminal points of the optic nerve can so vibrate in the brain as to give visions of form and colour of exquisite beauty, is a problem as yet beyond the power of science to solve; for how can the brain, which is itself but a mechanism of albumen and fat with some phosphorus, see and comprehend such things?

To myself it is much more difficult to conceive how *any mechanical* arrangement of albumen, fat, and phosphorus can know the glory and seek the mystery of the universe, than to believe that there is in man a faculty or auto-noetic power called thought, mind, or soul, which can, under peculiar conditions, and at rare intervals, see physical things independently of mechanical optics by a faculty called clairvoyance.

I have thus by examples of each stage of clairvoyance attempted to show how, step by step, we advance from simple thought-reading to deeper brain-reading, and from that to the still deeper diagnosis of internal bodily disease, hidden from the eye of sense, but revealed to the penetrating eye of the soul, and from that to the travelling of the soul to distances on this earth beyond optical vision, and thence to the highest powers of the soul as an independent mind, knowing the past, the present, and the future, and leading to that ultimate climax of the soul, whereby it ascends, as in holy entrancement, and enters the regions where the Immortals dwell.

Thus this intelligent power called soul, operates not only independently of the senses, but beyond the reach of the physical senses, and shows itself as an independent auto-noetic power, triumphing over pain and disease and death, and penetrating matter, and acting as if its connection with matter were but a passing accident.

And just as chemistry can show that there is no such thing as the destruction of matter, but only its ever-varying transformations; and just as physics can prove that although power may disappear in one place, it is only that it may reappear in another place, in obedience to the law of the Conservation of Energy, —so the soul of man, as a thinking and auto-noetic power—although its external clothing may pass through various transformations and regenerations—can be demonstrated as a *unity* incapable of the subdivisions of decay; and thus as an immortal life is destined to survive "the war of elements, the wreck of matter, and the crash of worlds."

We may sit in a darkened theatre before the act, and by some minute chink in the dark curtain which separates the audience from the stage, obtain a glimpse of the splendid spectacular luminosity which awaits us ; and I would ask, Do not the rare glimpses which clairvoyants sometimes obtain, perhaps reveal that there may be a world of light, as Milton says, "Above the din and stir of this dim spot which men call earth," to which the highest form of saintly entranced clairvoyance may possibly reach, and show "that some there be who by due steps aspire to lay their just hands on that golden key which opes the palace of eternity."

Thus the highest entranced soul knows, as an absolute fact, that materialism is not true. It beholds its immortal life, and in the innermost secret of its own essence, it listens to the still small voice of the eternal God.

XI.—ANÆSTHETICS,

AND THEIR REVELATIONS OF THE SOUL.

IN the year 1800, Humphrey Davy, then twenty-two years of age, suggested that the inhalation of nitrous oxide gas might be used in surgical operations as a means of preventing pain ; but it was not until 1844 that Mr. Horace Wells, a dentist residing at Hartford, Connecticut, used it in extracting teeth, and thus demonstrated the truth of Humphrey Davy's conjecture.

In the year 1846, Dr. Morton, of Boston, U.S., demonstrated for the first time that the severest surgical operations could be performed without pain under the inhalation of the vapour of sulphuric ether. Lastly, Sir James Simpson, of Edinburgh, in the same year, introduced the beneficent use of chloroform in the labours of child-bed.

Anæsthetics having thus conferred on poor suffering humanity the inestimable blessing of painless surgery, I ask with reverence and hope : Are anæsthetics not yet destined to confer on the human race the infinitely greater boon of scientifically demonstrating the existence, free from the body, of the human soul ?

It is true that the vast majority of human beings

do instinctively believe in the existence of the human soul; and this is of all arguments the strongest, because any spiritual belief, which is all but universal in the human mind, must be regarded as an instinctive revelation in harmony with the nature of man, and therefore true ; and when, further, this instinct is found to increase the happiness and welfare of the human race, the proof to me seems absolute, because no falsehood can produce ultimate good.

There are, however, among the scientific minds of the present day, an ever-increasing number of thoughtful, truthful, and benevolent men, who yet doubt or deny that there exists any entity or ego apart from the body, and these men assert that when the bodily organisation dies the man himself, so far as evidence goes, becomes extinct.

Let us then inquire whether or not this materialistic assertion is true, or whether the use of anæsthetics cannot demonstrate that this assertion of unbelief is contrary to fact.

It has been long known that persons who have been all but drowned, so as to appear actually dead, but who—it may be after hours of manipulation—have been restored to consciousness, have sometimes declared that the process of drowning, after the first struggle, was not agonising, but actually pleasurable.

These individuals have sometimes said that the entire history of their lives has flashed before them as if photographed instantaneously, and that then they have seemed to ascend to heavenly regions and celestial felicity.

Again, many of those who in the dentist's hands have inhaled nitrous-oxide, which produces asphyxia exactly analogous to that of drowning, have expressed their enjoyment of great spiritual happiness, even as their teeth were being extracted.

The same results have often followed the use of chloroform; and I myself, one day in the year 1874, while inhaling chloroform as a relief to the agony of passing a small renal calculus, suddenly, to my great wonder, found my ego, or soul, or reasoning faculty, clothed, and in the form of my body, standing about two yards outside my body, and contemplating that body as it lay motionless on the bed.

This startling discovery was to me most significant, and becoming suddenly awakened to its importance, I called on three medical men who had very large experiences in the giving of anæsthetics.

In reply to my question, one gentleman said, " I can quite believe your assertion, as I have often heard patients express a similar idea, although in a confused way." Another gentleman said, " He had himself on three occasions taken chloroform, and on each occasion he found himself, as it were, pleasantly whirling and soaring in the air "; and the third gentleman said, " My patients have often said that under my operations they felt no pain, but *saw* all I was doing like spectators looking on and watching the operations."

In connection with these facts concerning drowning and anæsthetics, I will here draw attention to what are called mesmeric experiments.

I have, since the year 1839, witnessed many mesmeric experiments, and I have found that certain individuals, while their minds have been concentrated on a physical point, and their breathing has thus become slower and slower, have passed into trance more or less profound, and while in this state it is well known from the evidence of Dr. Esdaile, of Calcutta, and others, that the severest surgical operations have been performed, not only without pain, but while the patient has at the same time passed into ecstatic joys.

The history of ecstatic martyrs has furnished additional evidence in this direction.

Thus we find in mesmeric trance a condition of things exactly analogous to what we sometimes find during the administration of anæsthetics.

Lastly, those who have studied Oriental Occultism know that there is an order of Hindu ascetics who, living lives of fasting, contemplation, and prayer, can so discipline their bodies as by practice to retain the breath until they become asphyxiated, and these ascetics assert that thus they can project their souls from the body, and, becoming entranced, ascend to God.

The Christian saints, without exactly practising the same method, so far as the breath is concerned, also at periods became entranced, and, "ascending to heaven, united their souls with the Lord."

Now all this is *one*.

Whether by drowning, asphyxiating gases, mesmeric trance, or "internal breathing," or the self-imposed asphyxia of the Hindu ascetics, or the entrancements of the ecstatic saints, the *modus operandi* is analogous and the result identical, namely, the temporary death through the absence of breath in the lungs, and thus the temporary freeing of the soul. As St. Peter says, "Dead in the body, but alive in the spirit."

This trance is dangerous if pushed too far by the operation of medicinal substances; but in the entrancement produced by mesmerism or ecstasy, the condition may exist for hours, days, or even weeks, while the ecstatic declares on his return to earth-consciousness that he has in spirit, outside his body, been in Paradise, and beheld things impossible to utter. Although St. Paul says that when caught up into Paradise he beheld things not lawful to utter, he knew not whether he was in or out of the body.

The sceptic will say all this proves nothing but hallucination and dreams.

In reply to this objection, I would say that trance is a condition entirely beyond mere sleep, and that visions of the spirit are entirely distinct from the dreams of imperfect sleep, and those who have been in trance know its intense reality.

No one in mere sleep can submit to painful operations, not only without flinching, but with the smile of joy on his face; and no one dreams that he is *outside* his body; he dreams that he is with his body. Moreover, those who awake from dreams at once admit the dream, but those who return from the revelations of entrancement assert that these were not dreams; and, therefore, sceptics who merely suggest explanations cannot have the weight of those who assert their beliefs from experience.

I therefore submit that sceptics have, in the use of anæsthetics, a physical and scientific means of testing the beliefs and assertions of pneumatologists as to the existence outside the body of the soul or ego as a scientific fact, capable of demonstration.

The sceptic will deny that the all but universal belief of human beings in the existence of the soul has any scientific weight. He will further deny the authority of spiritual revelations. He will discredit the experiments of mesmerists, and deny the assertions of Hindu or Christian ecstatics; but if he experiment with medicinal anæsthetics on his own person, he may find out, as I and others have done, that the soul may be projected outside the body, and externally exist as the true ego.

If thus the soul can be demonstrated as an

objective *fact*, the next step is to postulate that the ego, or soul, or mind is a *unity*.

All visible substances are compounds, and as compounds are liable to disintegration, decay, and death. Even the royal gold can thus, from its liability to slow decay, be shown to be not an elementary but a compound substance. But the soul as a *unity* is incapable of division, therefore incapable of decay, and is therefore immortal.

Finally, those who have demonstrated the existence of their spiritual nature, know that in so doing they have demonstrated to themselves the existence of the Father of all Spirit—God.

The publication of these views called forth the following interesting corroborations:—

"Many visions have been vouchsafed me, but I know of none that gave me the exquisite delight as that produced by an anæsthetic, and never did I so regret the awakening as on that occasion; and I feel now that I was then really temporarily, to all intents and purposes, dead in the body but alive in the spirit. "M.A. (Cantab.)"

"Since the publication of your article, a remarkable statement has been made to me by a gentleman to whom I had just administered an anæsthetic. Knowing my patient (an eminent literary reviewer and critic) to be of great intelligence, I asked him immediately on recovery to describe any sensations or impressions he may have experienced. With considerable earnestness and excitement he said (in nearly his own words), 'I thought I had *in some way, you know, got to the bottom and behind everything, saw the cause and reason of things, and understood the mystery of life and the great secret that all have sought.* And I called to others to put in writing what it was, and how I found it out, but I now remember nothing more than this.'

"WALTER H. COFFIN."

Further, Mr. Stodart, dentist, told me he had met with many analogous cases; and at the Dental Hospital they told me that the patients under gas often saw visions and spoke of being out of their bodies.

The above observations may be compared with those of Sir Humphrey Davy, who made a long series of experiments upon himself, to ascertain the effects of breathing nitrous oxide. About one of his earlier experiments he says:—

"I gradually began to lose the perception of external things, and a vivid and intense recollection of some former experiments passed through my mind, so that I called out, 'What an amazing concatenation of ideas!'"

In one of his later experiments Sir Humphrey Davy experienced the following sensations:—

"By degrees, as the pleasurable sensations increased, I lost all connection with external things; trains of vivid visible images rapidly passed through my mind, and were connected with words in such a manner as to produce perceptions perfectly novel. I existed in a world of newly-connected and newly-modified ideas. When I was awakened from this semi-delirious trance my emotions were enthusiastic and sublime, and for a minute I walked round the room, perfectly regardless of what was said to me. As I recovered my former state of mind I felt an inclination to communicate the discoveries I had made during the experiment. I endeavoured to recall the ideas; they were feeble and indistinct; one collection of terms, however, presented itself, and with the most intense belief and prophetic manner I exclaimed to Dr. Kinglake, ' *Nothing exists but thoughts!—the universe is composed of impressions, ideas, pleasures, and pains!*'"

On the assumption that anæsthetics occasionally separate the soul from the body, the above is an example how entrance into the spiritual state suddenly transformed one of the greatest physicists of modern times into an idealist.

Mr. A. Duguid, Kircaldy, reports:—

"My wife's mother, Mrs. Arnot, left us for the higher existence on Feb. 5th, 1880. There is a married daughter living at Banchory, three miles from this town; Mrs. Arnot died at *eleven* o'clock in the forenoon. The married daughter was very ill in labour, and the doctors in attendance thought it wise to administer chloroform. She passed under the influence thereof at *twelve* o'clock noon, and while doing so told all those present that her mother was dead, for she saw her, and that the baby was with her mother. No tidings of the mother's death reached the daughter's house till *four* o'clock in the afternoon, and on no account was she told after coming from under the influence of the chloroform. It is noteworthy that she spoke of having seen her babe in the spirit-world as well as her mother, which was quite consistent with fact, as the infant died in the doctor's hands, and was in the spirit-world while the mother was still under the influence of chloroform."

Another correspondent writes, " I took nitrous oxide and chloroform for two operations, and seemed to get behind the veil that covers creation, and I seemed to see unceasing energy working out the will of God."

An intimate friend also said to me, " I experimented with chloroform according to your suggestion, and I seemed to receive an absolute demonstration of the spirit-world. I further saw that spirit was the substance of matter, and that what we call matter was a mere shadow. So strong was this conviction, that, for days after my experience I could not restrain my laughter at the delusion that the things visible to the physical eyes were the real things."

These communications are strongly confirmatory of my views, and go to show that anæsthetics liberate the soul by, as it were, drowning the body, that is, by expelling the air from the lungs. That, in fact, they drive the soul out of the body and thus render the body incapable of experiencing pain, for it is by the mind that pain is known, and hence the lower the mental organisation in animals the less sensitive are their bodies to pain.

The expression used by Mr. Coffin's patient, when under anæsthesia, "that he had got to the bottom and behind everything, and saw the cause and reason of things, and understood the mystery of life and the great secret that all have sought," is the expression of the profound truths known to saints and ecstatics; while the expression used by Sir Humphrey Davy, when under the influence of nitrous oxide, that " nothing exists but thought," was a profound revelation of Divine Philosophy.

I would therefore urge on Scientists, Psychologists, and Materialists, further experiments with anæsthetics as a means of arriving at an experimental demonstration of the independent existence and powers of the human soul. And as probably not fewer than one thousand patients are daily put under anæsthetics in Europe and America, what an enormous amount of opportunity is offered for experiment.

XII.—MATTER:

ITS SPIRITUAL SUBSTANCES—A DEMONSTRATION.

THE phenomena of *the passage of matter through matter* has much interested Spiritualists. The facts are that during dark *séances*, while the circles are seated around tables and with joined hands, wooden and other rings being previously placed on the table, these have frequently been found threaded on the arms of those present, on the understanding and belief that continuity of joined hands remained unbroken.

In the presence of the medium Husk this has during the last twenty years been done probably a thousand times, and the feat, taking it for granted that all hands are at the moment joined, is obviously a physical impossibility.

On no occasion, however, up to a certain date, while I held any hand, was a ring ever placed either on my own arm or on the arm of the hand I held, and I therefore in those days suspected that in most, if not in all instances, when the act was accomplished, it was during a moment when two sitters inadvertently, and perhaps unconsciously, relaxed their grasp of each other's hands.

This explanation, however, was never admitted, either by the medium or by the sitters, and I was always told that my magnetism was of so positive a nature that the operation could not be performed either on my own arm or on that of any hand I held.

The subject interested me more than any other in Spiritualistic phenomena, for, if demonstrated, it would establish the fact that Matter was subject to Spirit, and then all other Spiritual phenomena would be easy to accept, and I therefore determined, if possible, to bring the question to a crucial test.

Accordingly I had an iron ring made of a size which made it impossible to force it over my own or Husk's hand, and this ring during four years I invariably carried in my pocket and placed on the table at the commencement of every *séance* I attended.

This ring, during four years, was repeatedly found on the arms of those present at *séances*, but on no occasion, up to a certain date, was it ever placed on my arm, or on that of any hand I held.

Still I persisted, because I was from time to time promised a demonstration if only I persevered.

I did persevere, and the promise was fulfilled on the evening of the 18th December, 1884, at the house of my friend Mr. Stuart-Menteath.

Mr. Menteath had arranged to hold a series of *séances* in his own house, with the medium Husk, and as far as possible always to have the same sitters present, and who should all be known to each other ;

and on the night of my ring demonstration, Mr. Menteath, Miss Menteath, Mrs. Fitzgerald, Captain James, General Maclean, the Rev. Mr. Newbold, and myself were present.

We sat as usual at the table, and the light being put out, a voice, apparently coming through Husk, said, " Dr. Wyld, we think we shall be able to put your ring on the medium's wrist to-night, so be sure and hold his hand securely."

To this I objected that the controls had always said that they could not pass the ring on to the arm of anyone whose hand I held, and that as I knew that no force could pass the ring over Husk's hand, I should be content not to hold his hand. The voice replied, "But we wish you to hold the medium's hand."

Accordingly I laid hold of Husk's left hand with my right hand, while Captain James held his right hand, and with my left hand I then cautiously examined Husk's forearm, but found no ring there. Then taking my ring in my left hand, and holding it, as directed, lightly with two fingers, I gave the remaining fingers of my left hand to my next sitter. The voice then said, " I will take the ring out of your hand, ring it three times on the table, and then place it on the medium's wrist."

The ring was then immediately taken from me, rung three times on the table, and placed round

Husk's wrist, while he uttered a cry as of pain, and struggled convulsively to free his hand from mine, but I held all the tighter, and with my left hand eagerly sought and found a ring on his left wrist, and called for a light, while I held the hand and wrist of Husk as in a vice.

When the light was produced we all saw the ring on the wrist, and all tried to remove it, but without success; while I satisfied myself by the examination of my private marks that the ring was my own ring; and I need scarcely say that my sensations of success, after so many failures during four years, were intense.

The evidence stated categorically is as follows:—
1. I have an ovoid ring made of hammered iron $\frac{5}{16}$in. thick, and privately marked, of a size I found impossible to force over my own or Husk's hand, as tested by myself and many others. 2. The measurements were: Internal long diameter, 2·75in.; short diameter, 2in.; internal circumference, 7·8in.; the circumference of Husk's left hand at the date of the experiment, as measured by a cord tightly tied round it, being 9·15in. 3. It is, of course, impossible, according to physics, to pass any body measuring 9·15in. through a ring measuring only 7·8in. internal circumference, and yet the feat was accomplished.

The ring on the wrist of Husk was certainly my ring, intact and untampered with. All present at the experiment tried to remove the ring from Husk's wrist, but found it manifestly impossible. I am, therefore, justified in stating this experiment to be a demonstration of the occult passage of matter through matter.

This ring suddenly fell from Husk's wrist to the ground, about an hour after it had been placed there; and I immediately picked it up and found it unaltered in any way, and I still have this ring in my possession.

On after experiments with this ring, I found that although too small to be forced over my hand or over Husk's hand, it could yet be forced, with some difficulty, over the hands of most ladies, and I therefore had my oval ring No. 2 made, with diameters about $\frac{3}{16}$ in. less than that of ring No. 1, and this ring could not be forced over the hand of any young lady on whom it had been tried.

I sent this ring to Husk, about the 26th January, 1885, and on the 28th, at his own house, the ring was, according to evidence, placed on Husk's wrist, while my friend, Mr. Bampfylde, held his hand.

I sat with Husk on the 29th, when he showed me my ring No. 2 on his wrist, and by the most minute examination, requiring the use of a magnifying glass, I satisfied myself with absolute certainty that it was my own ring No. 2, and Mr. Bampfylde assured me that he had handled my ring before the *séance* began, and immediately afterwards, while he held Husk's hand, it appeared on the wrist of Husk.

The sceptic may smile at my simplicity in permitting Husk to have possession of the ring beforehand, as it might enable him to make a duplicate, or tamper with it, but my object was to bring the ring and Husk's body magnetically *en rapport*, and my ring remained untampered with and no duplicate ring ever appeared.

Having got my ring No. 2 on Husk's wrist, it struck me that I should show it to Mr. Maskelyne, of the Egyptian Hall, as not only one who was interested in such matters, but as confessedly the most expert conjuror in England, if not in Europe. I did so, and he expressed himself as much interested and quite unable to account for the position of the ring on Husk's wrist. He admitted that the ring was soundly welded, and that it could not have been hot welded on the arm, and he suggested the possibility of cold welding, but admitted that that would require great pressure and considerable time. He also admitted that the ring, in his opinion, could not possibly be removed, or, if possible, not without great injury to Husk's hand.

Further, as Mr. Maskelyne suggested the possibility of removing the ring by force, if the shape of the ring corresponded with the form of the moulded hand in forcing the ring off; I being prepared for this suggestion, offered him a soft copper twisted wire ring I had made the exact size of the ring on the wrist, and which would readily take the ever changing form of the hand as the ring was withdrawn; but on seeing the small copper ring he wisely declined to make the attempt to pass it over Husk's hand. (*Light*, 10th April, 1885.)

Mr. Maskelyne subsequently said that a ring could be more easily forced over a hand than withdrawn from it, but this I know, from frequent practice, to be the reverse of the case, although the remark is true as applied to finger rings. And with regard to the suggestion of *cold* welding, every worker in iron will assert that my ring is hot welded.

The publication in *Light* of this experiment as "*A demonstration of the passage of Matter through Matter*" called forth many letters, but the late Edmund Gurney, one of the most acute and earnest members of *The Society for Psychological Research*, devoted his energies, in accordance with the well-known and almost excessive prudence of this Society, to an attempt to show that my experiment did not rank as a "*demonstration.*"

His arguments in various letters lay almost exclusively in the direction that I could not be absolutely certain of the identity of my rings with the rings which appeared on Husk's wrist. But as from fine marks of extreme minuteness and incapable of imitation, as well as from marks made secretly by myself, I was absolutely certain of the identity of my rings with those on Husk's wrist, Mr. Gurney's arguments thus fell to the ground.

But even were it impossible to prove the identity of the rings, that would not affect the case, which was simply this: "There is a ring on Husk's wrist, the presence of which cannot be accounted for by men of science, or by Maskelyne, the prince of jugglers, and I, knowing its history, pronounce its presence on Husk's wrist to be the result of occult force, and therefore '*a demonstration* of the passage of Matter through Matter.'"

The case continuing to create much attention, about a year after the above record, pressure was put on the Society for Psychical Research to submit the phenomenon to scientific investigation, and accordingly a committee was appointed, and on the 17th April, William Crookes, F.R.S., Victor Horsley, F.R.C.S., W. C. Bull, F.R.C.S., and A. T. Myers, M.D., met Husk at 24, Clarges Street, and subjected his hand and ring to careful examination and measurement. And their measurements of my ring, although they are slightly larger than my own, I am willing to accept as correct.

The verdict arrived at by the committee is in these words: "We cannot infer that it is impossible that the ring should have come into the position in which we found it by known natural means."

It will be remarked that this verdict is worded with

extreme caution, the double negative used being a form of words which usually implies an apologetic tone. But, however this may be, the verdict, gramatically considered, is contrary to the figures furnished by the committee itself, and this can be very easily and clearly shown.

Husk's hand was first moulded and then compressed with metallic tape, and subsequently with copper wire. The committee desired that he should submit to be etherised in order that they might apply crucial pressure, but as he declined to submit to this, three other men were found who submitted to the operation, and the committee seem to imply that had Husk submitted to this crucial operation, his hand might have been compressed so as to show the possibility of the ring being removed by natural means; but as the crucial experiments entirely failed to show this in regard to the three other cases, it may be fairly inferred that Husk's hand would not have been found an exceptional one.

Two of the men operated on had large hands, and these, as the ring was much smaller than their hands, I exclude, but man No. 3 had a hand, by a curious coincidence, almost identical in size with Husk's, but slightly a smaller hand.

The various measurements are given in millemetres, and are as follows, the measurements less than the ring in Husk's case being excluded :—

HUSK'S HAND WHEN COMPRESSED WITH METALLIC TAPE.	NO. 3 HAND WHEN SO COMPRESSED.
184	175
195	195
200	196
198	191

From these measurements it will be seen that Husk's hand, when compressed with metallic tape, was considerably larger than the hand of man No. 3 when so compressed.

HUSK'S HAND COMPRESSED WITH COPPER WIRE.	NO. 3 HAND WHEN CRUCIALLY COMPRESSED UNDER ETHER.
184	162
189	180
192	189
194	186

My ring measures 182-5, and from the measurements of Husk's hand it will be seen that they are all larger than that of the ring, and that two of the measurements of hand No. 3, when said hand was compressed to the utmost, are also larger than the ring.

The committee thus admit by their own figures that the ring could not possibly have been forced over hand, No. 3, and it is a most unwarrantable assumption that the ring could have been forced over Husk's hand, which was larger than hand No. 3, had he submitted to be etherised.

A true verdict therefore would have been in these words: "So far as our experiments have extended, they prove that the ring could not be removed from Husk's wrist without severe injury to his hand," this being the verdict of Mr. Maskelyne as above.

With regard to Husk having declined to submit to being deprived of his consciousness, when alone with strangers, who "were determined (as he said to me) that science should have the best of it," I think my readers will not be surprised at his prudence. I think the committee should have invited me to be present at their experiments, and had they done so I could not only have suggested tests which they seem to have omitted, but I think I could have induced Husk to submit to the action of ether, provided he were adequately remunerated for his trouble and risk.

But suppose it were granted that a soft copper ring could have been forced over a body larger in circumference than itself, which, of course, is absurd, it must be still more manifestly absurd to assert that a rigid iron ring which could not possibly be forced to take the ever varying form of the compressed hand in its progress towards removal, could have been removed intact.

Further, it was a strange omission on the part of the committee, on the supposition that the object was the discovery of truth and not the refutation of my "demonstration," that they did not, as I had done, construct a soft twisted copper wire ring the exact size of the iron ring on Husk's wrist, and try their best to pass it over his hand, for this copper wire ring would have much favoured the operation by taking in its progress onwards the ever changing shape of the compressed hand.

Had they tried this test they would have convinced themselves of its utter futility.

Finally, the reader must bear in mind that both Husk's hands were held at the moment the rings were placed on his wrist; although this part of the performance is unimportant, knowing as we do that the circumference of the ring being smaller than the circumference of the hand, its passage to the wrist by natural means was impossible.

As is well known, most remarkable instances of the passage of Matter through Matter are recorded in Zöllner's "Transcendental Physics" (as demonstrations of a *fourth dimension*, a phrase which is to me synonymous with the dynamic substance of matter), instances in themselves perhaps even more remarkable than the case of my rings. But the peculiarity of my case is, that whereas in every previous instance in which rings have been placed in positions impossible to physics, they have been at once, or very soon after the feat, removed; while my ring has been retained on Husk's wrist for nine years, as a standing evidence of occult work, and in this respect the case is, I believe, unique in the history of Spiritualism.

There is a well-known experiment in which, while

a disc with figures imprinted on it is made to revolve with immense velocity, a flash of electricity is thrown on the disc, when, due to the instantaneousness of the flash, the figures on the disc are seen as motionless ; and this experiment in its instantaneity resembles these ring feats.

The occult explanation of these astounding facts regarding iron and other rings, is, that Matter is composed of molecules coherent but not absolutely in contact, and that just as by heat substances can be vaporised, and by cold again condensed—heat dispersing the molecules through vibratory action—so spirit will force can do likewise, but with possibly enormously accelerated vibrations, or possibly the work is done by reversing the magnetic polarity of the atoms.

It must, however, be admitted that these wonders are impossible of belief except to those who *know* them as absolute facts, and therefore the experiments should, if possible, be repeated again and again, when suitable mediums can be found, for if the passage of Matter through Matter can be established widely as a fact, it must revolutionise the whole of science, and as the greater contains the less, make all other spiritualistic facts easy of belief, by the revelation of Spirit as the Substance of force and Matter.*

---

* For the benefit of those who may desire to see the ring on Husk's wrist, he may be heard of at the office of *Light*, 2, Duke Street, Charing Cross.

XIII.—BUDDHISM AND CHRISTIANITY CONTRASTED.*

WE have all heard much of late years of the parallel between the life and teachings of Gautama Buddha† and Jesus Christ ; but we have not heard so much about the contrasts in life and doctrine between these two founders of the two great religions of the world.

Most students of Buddhism have arrived at the conclusion that the morality taught by Gautama could scarcely be surpassed in excellence, but that his system might be a philosophy but could not be a religion in the accepted sense of that term, inasmuch as it denied the existence of a rational God or Creator, and consigned the *soul* of man, after successive and oblivious re-incarnations, to total extinction as a personality.

Believing, as I once did, that many Buddhists were *Theosophists*, that is, seekers after the wisdom of God, I could not then accept the atheistic and nihilistic interpretation of the teachings of the pure and gentle Gautama ; but the publication, by Trübner, of Colonel Olcott's " Catechism of Buddhism," seems to

---

* Reprinted from my letters in *Light*, 1882, and *The Spectator*.
† Sakya was the family name ; Muni, or the silent one ; Gautama the clan ; and Buddha means enlightened ; and so the full title is — The Lord Sakya-Muni Gautama The Buddha.

confirm these views, as hitherto expressed by Max Müller, Rhys-Davids, and other learned Orientalists.

I had always thought that *Nirvana* signified that rest in entrancement, through which the soul as an active consciousness, existed in God, but this Catechism of Buddhism entirely dissipates that idea.

In the second volume of Max Müller's "Selected Essays" may be found learned and interesting papers regarding Buddhism, and I now avail myself of the information thus given, in my present brief review of Colonel Olcott's Catechism.

This Catechism, although it contains only 28 pages, must be regarded as a work of considerable value and importance, because not only is it the first attempt to produce in English a Catechism or formal epitome of Buddhism, but because it, in a brief form, confirms the result of British Oriental scholarship, by the Buddhist High Priest of Adam's Peak, and Principal of the Buddhist College.

We may therefore accept of this Catechism as an authorised statement of the Buddhistic system as taught by the highest authorities in the Buddhist Church of Ceylon.

In studying this Catechism, the first thing that strikes us as surprising is the fact, that although Buddhists are *said* to number 500,000,000 (Monier Williams believes the true number to be under 300,000,000), and to have existed for 2,400 years, yet no Bible or Catechism of the system has hitherto ever been published for the instruction of the believers.

This forms a remarkable contrast to the fact that the Christian Bible has been translated into every important language or dialect in the world, and has been flooded over the world in millions.

Notwithstanding this Oriental apathy, Colonel Olcott, who we may take for granted now avows himself openly as a convert to Buddhism, with the enthusiasm of a recent convert, declares his belief that Buddhism, as the most scientific of all religions, is destined to become the religion of the whole world!

In his enthusiasm he gives the population of the globe as about 1,300,000,000, and the Buddhists being about 500,000,000 ; he adds—" not quite half the population of the earth."

But according to the most recent statistics the population of the globe is close on 1,500,000,000, and admitting that nominal Buddhists may number 500,000,000, we find them not " one-half nearly," but *one-third* exactly, of the inhabitants of the earth.

Of these 500,000,000 nominal Buddhists, nearly 415,000,000 are Chinese, thus leaving about 85,000,000 as the number of Buddhists residing in Siam, India, Thibet, etc.

Now of these supposed 415,000.000 Chinese, taken in the lump as Buddhists, we know very little ; but this we know, that in China there are three religions, those of Confucius, Laa-tsi, and Buddha, and that idol worship and the worship of Spirits and of forefathers is very common; and religion, as such, is considered of little serious importance; and if so, I think we may conclude that Chinese Buddhists have no very close resemblance to their founder, and that Chinese Buddhism is not likely to become the universal religion of the future.

The followers of Christ, on the other hand, number 390,000,000, and if we estimate the value of a religion by the physical, moral, and intellectual qualities of the nations holding it, we must arrive at very different conclusions to those of Colonel Olcott as to the religion of the future.

Buddhism has now existed on the earth for 2,400 years; but during that long period of the earth's history it has, with the single exception of its founder, produced not one man of great historic importance, not one who has affected the destiny of the human race.

Buddhism has not produced a single example of greatness in poetry, the arts, sciences, or literature, or even war.

No great painter, or poet, or thinker, or discoverer, or mechanic, or chemist, or geologist, or electrician, or astronomer.

No Plato, or Aristotle, or Galileo, or Copernicus, or Newton, or Watt, or Stephenson, or Kant, or Bacon.

No Phidias, or Apelles, or Raphael, or Michael Angelo, or Leonardo, or Murillo, or Rubens, or Velasquez, Reynolds, Hogarth, Rosa Bonheur, Landseer, Turner, Meissonier, or Millais.

No La Place, Franklin, Davy, Faraday, Lyell, Playfair, Fraunhoffer, or Darwin.

No Dante, Cervantes, Shakespeare, Milton, Goethe, Burns, Scott, Tennyson, Spinosa, or Dickens.

If so, then we ask—where is the intellectual material by means of which the world is to be converted to Buddhism?

It may be replied that Buddhism is the science of the soul, and that it has nothing to do with the arts and literature. But to this I would say that a true science of the soul must bring that soul *en rapport* with the Divine Spirit, the fountain of all knowledge and wisdom; and hence it is that the greatest discoverers in all ages of the world have been men deeply interested in Divine things. But as Buddhists ignore the Divinity, they have thus shut out the Divine sources of Inspiration.

In Colonel Olcott's Catechism, we are told that there is no personal God and no Creator, but that two things only are eternal, viz., *Akasa* and *Nirvana*, and that " everything has come out of this Akasa, in obedience to a law inherent in it."

Now this Akasa, so far as the Western mind can see, has its nearest equivalent in Magnetism, and for myself I believe that all physical nature has its foundation in Magnetism, and that the cohesive force in matter is magnetic force.

If so, then so far good; but whence came Magnetism, and how came it to be a law?

"The Buddhist," says Colonel Olcott, "cannot conceive of a Creator," but neither, I reply, can the Christian conceive of a self-created law of Akasa.

But Colonel Olcott says, "Nirvana is eternal," and he thus describes that unthinkable quantity—

"Nirvana is a condition of total cessation of changes—of perfect rest—of the absence of desire, and illusion, or sorrow, of the total obliteration of everything that goes to make up the physical man."

"Before reaching Nirvana man is constantly being reborn; but, when he reaches Nirvana, he is reborn no more."

This definition of Nirvana is sufficiently positive, but Max Müller gives a discussion between a teacher and a scholar. The scholar asks, "Does Nirvana exist, and if so, where is it?" To which the teacher replies, "The position of Nirvana cannot be defined any more than you can define the position of the flame of a candle which is blown out."

Now, if Nirvana is eternal, and *a condition of perfect rest*, how came it to exist, and how can it be said to exist at all, seeing that existence can only be philosophically conceived as an active or passive force?

And, if it is "*as a flame blown out,*" how this extinguished flame can, with the assistance of Akasa, create worlds and work out man's perfection, is surely a puzzle beyond unravelling by the Western mind.

But if, before Nirvana arrives, man is "*constantly being reborn*" in all possible and troubled forms, and with total unconsciousness of all previous individualities, one can scarcely be surprised that he should long for an ending to all this phantasmagoria by a final rest in total abnegation!

In answer to Question 122, "Does Buddhism teach the Immortality of the Soul?" the answer is, "Everything, man included, is subject to change. That which is subject to change cannot be permanent, and so there can be no immortal survival of a changeful thing like the soul."

But "man's unsatisfied desires at death," the "last yearnings of the dying person" are reborn as a new aggregation or individuality.

This survival of "*the last yearnings*" of the dying man, as an individuality, might be accepted as the Hebrew doctrine that "as the tree falls so it lies," were it not that we are informed that these materialised last yearnings have no recollection of their paternity, nor have the *constantly* reiterated or re incarnated "*last yearnings*" any remembrances until Nirvana is arrived at. But as Nirvana has been described as if it were a condition of obliteration, it is not explained why remembrances should at such a moment only be possible; this Nirvana being, according to its Sanscrit derivation, simply "a blowing out."

Now, as to those who are destined to arrive at the ultimate knowledge of this Nirvana, the Catechism seems contradictory, for, in reply to Question 72, it is said, "A Buddhist is a being who, in some future birth, is sure to appear on earth as a Buddha"; but, in reply to Question 76, it is said, "It is not in the nature of every man to become a Buddha, for a Buddha is developed only at long intervals, when absolutely required as a teacher to show the forgotten path to Nirvana, but every being may equally realise Nirvana by conquering ignorance and gaining wisdom."

In reply to Question 69, it is said, "True science *entirely* supports this doctrine of Re-Incarnation as cause and effect, for science teaches that man is the result of a law of development from a lower to a higher evolution," but I suspect Mr. Darwin would rather stare at this application of his doctrine.

But, further, this law of evolution does not in any way support the mystical idea of Re-Incarnation; the entire argument of evolutionists being founded on the conduct of the *natural* law of generation.

It is somewhat curious that a catechism of

Buddhism should omit its Decalogue, or what may be called the Ten Fundamental Laws of Morals, but I give them as follows, from Max Müller's volume :—
1. Do not kill.
2. Do not steal.
3. Do not commit adultery.
4. Do not lie.
5. Do not get intoxicated.
6. Abstain from unsuitable words.
7. Abstain from public spectacles.
8. Abstain from excess in dress.
9. Do not have a large bed.
10. Do not receive silver or gold.

By way of comparison I add the Ten Commandments given by Moses, one thousand years before Buddha was born :—
1. The Lord thy God is one Lord, and thou shalt love the Lord thy God with all thy heart, and soul, and mind.
2. Thou shalt not worship graven images.
3. Thou shalt not take the name of God in vain.
4. Thou shalt sanctify and rest on the Sabbath.
5. Thou shalt honour thy father and mother.
6. Thou shalt not kill.
7. Thou shalt not commit adultery.
8. Thou shalt not steal.
9. Thou shalt not bear false witness (lie).
10. Thou shalt not covet the things of others.

It will be thus observed that the laws against adultery, murder, falsehood, and theft are the same in both Decalogues.

The Buddhist Decalogue has the advantage over that of Moses in denouncing intoxication, foolish words, and extravagant dress, but when it denounces all public spectacles it is surely weak; when it denounces the use of gold and silver it is in error; and when it denounces a large bed it is simply foolish. As if a selfish immorality could not be cultivated on a small bed, and a high Spiritual life be compatible with a large bed. But the wonderful characteristic distinction between the two Decalogues is that Buddha entirely ignores God, while Moses enunciates the grand doctrine of the unity of God.

The life of Gautama Buddha and his moral code were self-denying, pure, and beautiful, and Rhys-Davids says:—" The edicts are full of lofty righteousness—obedience to parents, kindness to children and friends, mercy towards the lower creation, indulgence to inferiors, reverence towards Brahmans, suppression of anger, passion, and cruelty and extravagance; generosity, tolerance, and charity."

All this is always admitted, but when Colonel Olcott says, " It is a *peerless* code of morals, and no man who ever existed sacrificed so much for our sakes," he says that which is easily disproved.

Even Moses, who lived in a dark age *one thousand*

years before Buddha, teaches a lofty righteousness, obedience to parents, mercy and rest for the brute creation, kindness and rest for servants and for the stranger in the land, and he lived and died for his people, accepting nothing for himself.

Buddha beautifully says, "A man who foolishly does me wrong I will return to him the protection of my ungrudging love ; the more evil comes from him the more good shall go from me," and thus Buddhists claim priority for Gautama over Jesus in propounding the law of forgiving and loving enemies.

Moses, however, as is not generally known to superficial students of the Bible, one thousand years before Buddha, says, Leviticus, xix., 18, "Thou shalt not avenge nor bear any grudge against the children of thy people, but thou shalt love thy neighbour as thyself and be kind to strangers, remembering that thou wast a stranger in the land of Egypt."

But Jesus goes far deeper, and with greater power says, " I say unto you love your enemies, bless them that curse you, and do good to them that hate you, and *pray* for them who despitefully use you and persecute you."

How, then, can Colonel Olcott call the code of Gautama a peerless code, and how can he say that " no man who ever existed sacrificed so much for our sakes "?

It is true that Gautama was a king's son, and

forsook a palace for a cave in order that he might study his own soul and preach truth and righteousness.

But is it so great a sacrifice to forsake the luxury, and indolence, and languor, and *ennui*, and bad health, and discontent of an Eastern Zenana and a walled garden, in order that one shall reach freedom, and obtain the inestimable wealth of Spiritual knowledge, wisdom, and power?

Hundreds of Christian ascetics have done in like manner, and although Gautama forsook a palace for the woods and caves, he was yet surrounded by loving and adoring disciples. He lived a contented life, and died a quiet and peaceful death.

How different it was with Jesus, with One who, although born in a manger, could easily, by His Spiritual wisdom and power, have made Himself King of the Jews, and could then by His power have driven the hated Romans into the sea and made Himself master of the world.

But He refused this life when it was within His reach; He refused the kingdoms of the earth when offered to Him, and lived as a wanderer, having nowhere to lay His head. He lived a life of incessant anxiety and toil; cured innumerable sick and diseased and devil-possessed people; taught the most perfect religion and morality; but was for ever in danger of His life, and was ultimately scourged, spit upon, and crucified. Compared with this, the grandest life of self-sacrifice that has appeared on this earth, the life of Gautama was but as a dreamy and quiet Epicureanism.

Some Buddhists I have met have not only questioned the existence of Jesus as a historic fact, but have even asserted His non-existence, on the ground, partly, that the oldest Christian MSS. date no earlier than the fourth century, thus leaving a hiatus of 300 years for the growth of the Myth!

I venture to assert that no man who has strong individuality of charater could ever doubt the fact of the historic Jesus. Men may invent subtleties, and reason from their doubts, but the quality of individuality in the mind reveals the truth in history.

For myself, I have no doubt whatever of the historic Gautama, for I hold it to be impossible that, say, 300,000,000 of human beings could continue to worship a code, unless derived originally from a living and visible man.

At the same time, it will surprise some of my readers to know, on the authority of Max Müller, that very few Sanscrit MSS. are older than four or five hundred years, and none older than the ninth or tenth century—that is, from 1,600 to 2,000 years after the death of Gautama.

That he existed as a man I have no doubt, but I question very much whether the doctrines given by this kindly and simple mind had any very exact resemblance to the incomprehensible doctrines contained in the hundreds of folios of Buddhistic MSS. Probably they have no more authority than our monkish legends of the dark ages.

Buddhism no doubt teaches a beautiful system of morals, and Gautama, the Buddha, was doubtless a good and a great man; but Buddhism as now propounded cannot be called a religion in any sense of that word.

It denies the existence of a rational God, and gives in His place a form of Magnetism and Negation.

It has no idea of what is called holiness, and it addresses no prayers to any being higher than man's inner nature, and it denies the immortality of the individual man or soul.

And this is the system Colonel Olcott prefers to the perfect moral and Spiritual teachings of the Christ, and is the religion which he believes is to become the religion of the future!

Buddha taught morality as a way to self-annihilation; Christ taught morality as a way to God and perfect happiness.

Buddha promises Nirvana, or "a blowing out," as man's highest destiny; Christ, through His disciples, promises immediately at death a happiness which "eye hath not seen nor ear heard, nor hath it entered into the heart of man to conceive,"—a promise which those who, while on earth, have ascended in holy trance, have frequently experienced, and thus proved.

The doctrines of Re-Incarnation and Nirvana explain how it is that Eastern Theosophists obstinately deny, in the face of innumerable facts, the reality of embodied Spirits ever appearing on this earth.

But possibly the Buddhism of Colonel Olcott and the Ceylon High Priest, may no more represent the truest and highest Buddhism, than ordinary verbal Christianity resembles the mystic and esoteric teachings of the Christ.

Finally I would ask, how can Buddhists call themselves Theosophists?

The meaning of that term is, *one who seeks the wisdom of God :* but if there is no Spiritual God and no Creator who is our Regenerator, and no being more personal than Nirvana, then the term *Theosophist* is absurd.

The term Theosophist does not occur in Buddhistical MSS., but is chiefly Christian, and Jacob Böhme is called the great Christian Theosophist.

He was a man who had all the moral qualities of Gautama In trance he had revealed to him the nature of matter, of man, of Christ, and of God, and he for ever declares from personal knowledge that Christ in man is eternal life. He knew that "Blessed are the dead who die in the Lord," and as he departed this life the harmony of the heavens was opened to him, and calling on the Lord Christ and on the Lord

God of Sabbaoth, he yielded up in peace and happiness his living soul.

So far then, as one can comprehend these teachings of the so-called Theosophists of the Atheistic Buddhist school, they are, that the soul and spirit are evolutions from matter, and that the supreme knowledge which saves the soul can only be acquired by the innermost self-introspection, and herein lies the great contrast between this form of Buddhism and Theism and Christianity. In this form of Buddhism there are no such words or thoughts as " Lead me to the rock which is higher than I "; or, " Father, into Thy hands I commend my spirit " ; or, " Our Father, who art in heaven "; or, indeed, any belief in any intelligence higher than the highest celestial man.

The moral teachings of Gautama Buddha and of Jesus Christ, are closely allied as to purity, love, and self-denial ; but on the other side, while there is no allusion by Buddha to a supreme intelligent First Cause, the continual teaching of Jesus is the personality and Fatherhood of God ; and hence I conceive it is that while Buddhism, having no external elevating force as its attraction upwards, has more and more become degraded into the lowest superstition and formalism, while Christianity, having, in direct communication with its centre the attractive force of a Divine love from above, must for ever be drawn upwards, and thus develop by evolution, those nations in the direct ratio of their living belief.

The great interest at present taken in Buddhism has arisen out of the recent researches of Oriental scholars, and more immediately from the influence of that beautiful poem, " The Light of Asia." A large proportion of thoughful people have become dissatisfied with the conventionality and formality of much Christian teaching, and Buddhism has been presented to these minds in a form pretending to be philosophical, and by the poem, in a lovely form; and the consequence has been that many who were indifferent or agnostical, have found in Buddhism, so presented, a vague form of faith which has pleased their imaginations. But the Buddhism of "The Light of Asia" has no resemblance to the practical Buddhism of Thibet, China, or Japan, where it has, as I have said, become degraded into the lowest forms of superstition and formality, as, for instance, in the praying-wheels of individuals and of communities, and in the elevation of gigantic phallic emblems in stone and metal in places of public resort in China and Japan, and in China by the destruction of female children. It is not denied that Christianity in the Middle Ages also descended to the lowest depths of superstition and formality; but in the midst of the vilest periods of the Christian Church, arose men like Michael Angelo, Raffaele, and Dante; while this very degradation of the Church was the cause of the rebound to a higher order of things under Luther.

Buddhism, however, having no internal or external force of reaction, has not and cannot ever arise out of its ashes; and it is, we repeat, very noteworthy that, beyond Gautama himself, out of Buddhism during the last 2,400 years, as I have already said, has arisen no prophet, no poet, no artist, no musician, no man of science, no discoverer, and not even one warrior of renown, or any regenerator of our race, while it is a formalism almost exclusively confined to the Mongolian race, the least spiritual of all the races of men.

Buddhism becomes transcendent in "The Light of Asia"; but Jesus has always been in the Sermon on the Mount, "The Light of the World"; and even a Shakespeare, had he attempted to turn into an epic the words of the Divine and miraculous Son of Man, could have attempted no more than "to gild refined gold."

Mr. Lillie, however, shows by many quotations from important MSS. that many Buddhists believe in a personal God; in saints living in Paradise; in the efficacy of prayer to God and to the saints; while Nirvana is described, not as an abstract idea, but as a place or paradise for the blessed.

In illustration of these views I make the following quotations from his book. With regard to God and prayer to God, it is said:—

"Those who follow religious observances shall be taught to follow in the right way and give glory to God."

"In Buddha God was revealed in the form of Mercy."

"Adi Buddha is without beginning; he is perfect and pure, the essence of wisdom and truth. He knows all and is ever present. He tenderly loves those who serve him. He is the Creator of all the Buddhas, *and of Akasa*. He is the God of Gods."

"O! the happiness of seeing the Holy One."

"I adore the perfect Buddha. I offer to him and I confess my sins."

"If I have sinned, may Buddha forgive my sins."

King Asoka, 250 years after Sakya-Muni, says: "I pray that all with me may attain unto eternal salvation."

Another says: "O that Sakya-Muni and our merciful Father would descend and be present with us."

As to the personality of the immortal life, Gautama-Buddha promised to reappear to his disciples, and he is said to have many times reappeared as a person.

As to Nirvana, it is thus described:—

"Those who keep the laws of the heavens have happiness in this life and in the next."

"Exert thyself to obtain the inner quickening, and when once freed from sin thou shalt reach the world of beauty."

"He who virtuously preaches the law of eternal life shall himself obtain Nirvana."

"Once freed from sin thou shalt reach the Divine world of the saints"—which is described as a *place*.

These extracts are sufficient to prove that many Buddhists believe in a personal God, in prayer, and in a conscious life in a future happy abode, and, indeed, we know that a conscious life after death is an all but universal belief of mankind.

In recent years the phrase "Esoteric Buddhism" has got into circulation, but regarding this invention of Madame Blavatsky, I agree with Rhys Davids that "it is neither Esoteric nor Buddhism," and to me it would be as correct to speak of esoteric pills and an esoteric police as to call this fantastic picture of Hindoo cosmogony esoteric.

The system says "There is no Creator, personal or impersonal, for physical matter must have had a physical cause, and what we call soul and spirit are only stages of matter in evolution, and what we call God is only transcendental matter in motion."

Thus it was described to me by an adept, who, moreover, in relation to reincarnation as its fundamental doctrine, said, "The Mahatmas have *reason to believe* that man has been reincarnated on this earth for 70,000,000 of years, and yet without any recollection of any period of this existence."

But when these enormously absurd Oriental figures were used, it must surely have been in the female sense of a million, only signifying a large number of years, for our geologist tells us that they only ask for a period of about 100,000 years, more or less, since man appeared on this planet.

XIV.—DARWINISM AND EVOLUTION.*

> That God, which ever lives and loves :
> One God, one Law, one Element,
> And one far-off Divine event,
> To which the whole creation moves.

THE teaching of Darwin that the evolution from the lower to the higher forms in plants and animals is due to the variability of organisms, the *struggle for existence and the survival of the fittest*, is with the reservation of certain "modifications" accepted by the great majority of scientific minds in Europe and America. As Thomson, in his "Study of Animal Life," says, "Evolution by natural descent, with modifications, is the order of Nature and is Darwinism and truth, yet, as Wallace says, the relative importance of the various factors in evolution is still very uncertain."

The influence which Darwin has had on the scientific study of natural history is immense, and as we contemplate his fine statue in the Natural History Museum at South Kensington we seem to see Socratic sagacity and persistent individuality ; and theologians now admit that geology, by the discovery of beds of extinct animals, has proved that the

---
* Reprinted from *Light*.

animals now occupying this earth, are not the primitive species of animals which they formerly have described as created by God and named by Adam. Nearly all, then, admit the fact of evolution in Nature, but the relative value of the factors in this evolution is still discussed by the best minds.

Wallace and Darwin simultaneously, but unknown to each other, arrived at the same idea regarding the evolution by "Natural Descent" in plants and animals, but these two great naturalists are not entirely at one; for while Wallace may be said in some respects to be more Darwinian than Darwin in regard to bodily evolution, he differs from Darwin when the latter teaches that the origin of the intellectual and moral faculties in man can be accounted for by physical evolution, which Wallace contends to be impossible.

Wallace says that the anatomical facts "amount almost to a demonstration that man in his bodily structure has been developed from some ancestral form common to man and the anthropoid apes," but "to a spiritual world we must refer, not only the complex forces which we know as gravitation, chemical force, and electricity, without which the universe as at present could not exist, and without which the religious, moral, and mathematical faculties of man are inexplicable."

And here we may say that the resemblance

between the highest apes and the lowest men (in whose body Thompson says may be found "a museum of some seventy relics of lower animal life") is truly appalling; but perhaps not more so than is the narrow difference physically between the idiotic or insane man and the man of sound mind.

Lamarck, the great French naturalist (1744-1829), about eighty years before the publication of the "Origin of Species" (1859), says: "There is a primary or predominant cause, which gives to animal life the power of progressive organization, in connection with the needs of its surroundings, and new parts are evolved by efforts from within."

That is, according to Lamarck, animals have, during unknown ages, been modified in their structure by the formative power of their constitutional tendency to progressive organization, which seems to me to imply a reasoning prearrangement called into action by the environment; while Darwin says the origin of species arises from the variability ever occurring in plants and animals, and the survival of the fittest in the struggle for existence.

Thus, Darwinism seems to me evolution, according to fitness in physical law, while Lamarckism is evolution, caused by the creative power of the mind; and it is interesting and important to know that there is a Neo-Lamarckism now engaging the thoughts of some of the best naturalists in Europe and America.

In the light of these divergent ideas it seems scarcely accurate to compare Darwin's law in biology with Newton's law in physics, for Newton's law is based on exact mathematics, while Darwin's law is based on a chain of evidence, of which some of the links in illustration are still missing and may never be found.

With regard to Man, for instance, the skull of the highest ape is bestial, while that of the lowest tribe of men is altogether human, and, making allowance for a few, possibly idiotic skulls, of prehistoric man, generally comparable in size and form with the average skull in all parts of the world. But as the ape's skull could not, according to Darwin, reach by evolution an equality with that of Man for probably hundreds of thousands of years, and if so, should have strewn the earth with degrees of its development in progressive evolution, sceptics have asked, " Where are the missing links ? "

To this great question the Darwinians have replied, " We have not yet explored one ten-thousandth part of the later geological strata, and one day the missing links will be found." For myself, I cannot resist the terrible suspicion that the highest ape may be my distant relative, but the non-appearance, not only as skeletons, but even as examples now living in remote valleys and hills, of the missing links, is still to me also suspicious. I have, however, no alternative to offer, except the suggestion, on which I do not rely, that knowing as I do that Spiritual beings can suddenly appear and disappear as strong, active, and reasoning men, the primitive Adamic man might have had an angelic origin, and that the higher apes may be degraded men, notwithstanding the missing links in their descent. And here I might remark that the absence in man of the hairy clothing of the ape, seems to me a difficulty, for the primitive man, if he came from the ape, would at first live in trees or caves, and could not have had a more fitting clothing than hair, in hot, cold, or wet weather; and the more hairy he was the more he would survive as the fittest in the struggle for existence, with his fellows and with wild beasts; while the absence of hair in the naked negro proves that man's nakedness has not arisen from wearing clothes.

Then the origin of consciousness, without which there could be no evolution, and the origin of the organs of sense, can hardly come under the category of *variations* and the survival of the fittest, and Darwin himself, up to the last, used to say that he "could not contemplate the difficulty of accounting for the first organ of vision without a cold shudder." It is true that younger Darwinians attempt to account for the growth of the eye by the accidental presence of a patch of pigment as a first step. But why more than one eye? why only two? and why always symmetrical? and why not occasionally a third eye looking backwards as a protection from the pursuing enemy springing from behind? And does not the presence of two eyes and their beautiful symmetry, suggest that ever recurring duality in nature, of some universal idea: emphatically represented in the numerical equality of the sexes, the solution of which mystery is impossible to science. But as I know there is a faculty of clairvoyance in which man sees better without his physical eyes, I can readily conceive of eyes being gradually created by the desires of the animal for light.

Then no evidence exists, on temple wall or elsewhere, that, except under artificial cultivation, any new species has arisen on the earth during the period of historic man, say seven thousand years; nor any change of form in that direction in animals; and although seven thousand years is, geologically considered, a short period, yet it is sufficient time to admit of appreciable changes in proportions; while human skulls, possibly 100,000 years old, found in caves, with the remains of extinct mammals, are of the same type as those of our day.

That enormous changes did occur in the plants and animals of this earth is, however, beyond question, and therefore these must have arisen, when through heat, moisture, or other causes, the growth of plants and animals must have been immensely accelerated.

That all the Mammalia may have come from a common ancestor is conceivable, and therefore, it is not inconceivable that the mouse and the elephant may have had a common ancestor. But it is not conceivable that the Crustacea and the Insectivora can have had the same ancestor as the Mammals, nor that the mosquito and the lady-bird, for instance, could have had any common ancestor with the whale, the eagle, or the leech, or indeed that these animals can even have a distant cousinly relationship.

Further, Wallace says: "The remarkable difference between varieties and species with respect to fertility when crossed is perhaps the greatest of all the difficulties," and in a chapter of thirty-four pages he attempts to answer these difficulties, but the explanation given, he admits, is very difficult for the reader to understand, and I confess myself as yet unable to unravel it.

Then there exists the dispute as to the influence of heredity, for while Weismann, who is followed by most Darwinians, denies the heredity of acquired characters, Spencer and others, believe in the heredity of acquired characters as a factor in evolution. Again, when we find that within a short century the form and voice of the inhabitants of the United States has so much altered from that of the typical Briton, we are impressed with the idea that the influence of climate and environment has not been sufficiently recognised. Lastly, instincts, which some regard as obtained by evolution, others would regard as mental causes of evolution. The one view may be regarded as physical, the other as metaphysical.

With these admitted differences and difficulties before us, although no untrained biologist can without presumption dogmatically urge opinions contrary to the Darwinians' fundamental law, and especially in its details, yet it is open to all sincere minds seeking truths—and especially, as even Weismann says: "To this day it is impossible to demonstrate the process of natural selection in its details in any one point"—to formulate their views, and I therefore venture to present the following argument :—

There was a time when this planet was a molten mass, during which time no vegetable or animal life could exist on its surface.

In the course of millions of years a crust of crystalline rocks became consolidated, and cooled sufficiently to admit of the condensation of steam into rain, rivers, and seas. These seas, rivers, and rain, assisted by air and wind, during an indefinite time, triturated the rocks and formed mud, and, in due course, out of this mud first vegetable and then animal life appeared.

The cause of the origin of this life on the planet is entirely beyond the scope of our recognised sciences ; and yet life appeared, and filled this earth with plants, animals, activity, life, mind, and beauty.

DARWINISM AND EVOLUTION.

Matthew Arnold would name the cause of this "The Eternal, not ourselves, that makes for Righteousness." Thomson calls it "The Almighty Volition as a Continuous Reality"; and the Hebrew Cosmogonist says: "The Spirit of God moved on the face of the waters, and said, 'Let the waters and the earth bring forth grass, and fish, and birds, and beasts, and man in Our image, with dominion over all the earth.'"

It is impossible to doubt that the cause of this planet must be the same cause as caused all the life on the planet.

The physical cause of the planet and its motion is the action of attraction and repulsion, or gravitation, and this law is known to exist throughout the universe of stars.

But, although the stars exist and move in accordance with this law, yet the forces which rule the earth and stars must be themselves ruled by their cause, that is, by Absolute Reason and Will.

If so, that Reason and Will must be as universally present as the forces of Nature are, and just as the smallest pebble on our shores is acted on by, and reacts on, the fixed stars, in a certain relation to size and distance, so also must the ever-present Reason and Will, or Mind, act on all Life or Mind, from that of the lowest cell to the highest organisation.

Logically that must be so, and thus the ultimate

cells of protoplasm and all plants and animals having Life or Mind, must have sensation, and if sensation they must have desires, and those desires or actions of Mind, must act on and be acted on by the Infinite Mind, in as exact a ratio as that of the universal force of physical Nature ; and thus every atom of Life or Mind is *en rapport* with the Infinite Mind.

If so, then the desires of cells and of complete animals, must be as cries to this " Infinite Hearer and Answerer of Prayer," and thus we arrive at the logical reason for a universal evolution in Matter, and in Mind, and thus all forms are Creations, or Ideas miraculously realised : in the sense that miracle is the action of spirit on matter.

The standpoint of this paper is that Force, or Motion, as in Lord Kelvin's theoretic vortex rings, as ultimate atoms, is the Substance of Matter, and Spirit is the Substance of Force, and the facts of experimental Psychology, as recorded in many volumes, go to demonstrate this statement.

In accordance with this view it is conceivable that the highest apes might, by gradual increase of brain in the direction of the moral and religious regions of the cerebrum, caused by higher and higher desires, ultimately grow a brain of that size and form, which admitted of the manifestation by influx, of the Spiritual as in Man, and evolution in this sense is a gradual and ceaseless Miracle, or action of Spirit on Matter.

Phrenology is not now so much heard of as in the days of George Combe, sixty years ago, but in the pages of its now extinct journal, may be read many illustrations of the gradual, and general or local increase in size of the human brain, by devotion to general or special mental culture; and if so, the action of Mind over Matter is thus illustrated, and the heredity of acquired habits rendered probable.

But although I regard Mind as the fundamental factor in Evolution, yet not the less can I admit that in "the struggle for existence and the survival of the fittest" we have a *secondary* factor, which, as a machinery, or method, aids the wishes of Nature in the production of higher forms.

XV.—REINCARNATION.

The doctrine of Reincarnation has existed in the East from the earliest times, and it is the fundamental doctrine of Buddhism; but it is a doctrine which has no existence in the Hebrew or Christian scriptures: and no Christian Seer or Saint ever held it, and I think it can be easily shown to have no foundation in reason, and indeed, to admit of an easy refutation by arithmetic.

Its advocates urge that justice demands reincarnation, because one life is far too short to experience all things, and because justice further demands that those who have had miserable lives, should have other chances of happiness.

The fact that there may be hundreds of millions of people on the earth who believe in reincarnation is no more an argument in its favour, than the equally wide belief that vengeance is the chief characteristic of the Creator, upholds that doctrine.

An unanswerable difficulty exists in the fact that of all the hundreds of millions who have believed in the doctrine, not one has ever had any memory of the details of any past life, as substantiated by a knowledge of the details of the archeology or history of their previous existences, while the vague ideas of supposed recollections, as Swedenborg points out, are due to imperfectly remembered visions in sleep.

That the happiness of men and women is most unequal on this earth (although far from so unequal as is supposed from the differences in their social positions) is no argument in favour of reincarnation, because one hour of celestial happiness might be sufficient to make amends for fifty years of earthly misery. And if there be no recollection of past evil deeds, there can be none of that remorse felt by the reincarnated, leading them to repentance and a higher life. Lastly, as man when on the spirit plane has the potentiality of all knowledge, successive reincarnations as a means of training, would be comparative foolishness.

Then the obliterating of all personalities and the confusing of all individuality, is a sufficient objection to the doctrine, while the fraud committed on parents whose children are not their own, but are only bodies inhabited by more or less degraded foreign souls, is surely the utmost of injustice ; and, moreover, what becomes of the souls which occupied their bodies before the restless spirits drove them out and took possession.

The doctrine, in its details, is the height of absurdity, for one good lady told me that she believed in reincarnation because men would be reborn as women, and thus justly suffer the pains of maternity! Another lady said to me she was ready to be reborn as a murderer, in order to experience its sensations; while a learned Buddhist told me that the Mahatmas "had reason to believe" that man had been reincarnated on this earth for 70 millions of years, and that, although the utmost which geologists ask for as the period of man's residence on this planet is about 100,000 years, more or less.

That earth-born souls may be reincarnated in other planets with new bodies may be true, but that all souls are reincarnated in the bodies of other people's children on this planet, is easily shown to be arithmetically impossible.

For instance, let us suppose that within say seventy years of the first appearance on this planet of men and women, there were 100 individuals living and no deaths. Then whence came the souls to these 100 men and women. Of course they must have come by ordinary generation, for to say they came from other planets is only to beg the question, and would only remove the difficulty one stage back.

But further, there has been an ever increasing number of human beings on this planet, and again I would ask, from whence came the ever increasing number of souls?

The command was to man to increase and multiply, and replenish the earth and subdue it, and now we have 1,500 millions of human bodies with souls residing on this earth; and surely common sense teaches us that they have been individualised in the ordinary process of generation, and hence the sacredness of marriage, because thereby immortal souls are created.

Strange to say, there are a few English men and women who profess to believe in reincarnation, although I have found that most of the women who said they believed in it, expected that they themselves would be the exceptions.

The Buddhist believes in reincarnation because he thereby hopes to escape from his personality, and ultimately to plunge into an abyss of nothingness.

The Christian believes that his individuality will exist for ever, in a spiritual world of ever progressing wisdom, goodness, and happiness.

XVI.—SLEEP AND TRANCE.

ALTHOUGH sleep has been the universal experience of man from his first creation until now, science has yet remained entirely ignorant of its mechanism, beyond the phrase that it is "a suspension of the sensory and motor functions," a materialistic statement which throws no light on the mystery.

If, however, we admit the teaching that man has a soul inhabiting his body, we then can at once see that the absence of this soul from the body must be the sleep or rest of that body.

The *suddenness* with which we often fall asleep, as at the fireside after dinner, or over a dull book after tea, is to most men and women a never-ending wonder; and although the sleep may be so sudden as to occur even in the middle of a word we may be reading, and the awaking as instantaneous, yet in that brief interval we are often conscious of dreams as of another form of life, in which we find the mind as active as in the waking state, but influenced as by strange and illogical surroundings.

At other times, during deep sleep, our dreams may be beautiful, and even prophetic, and the conclusions the Spiritualist arrives at are that sleep in such cases is due to the departure of the soul from the body, and dreams are foolish, confused, horrible, logical, beautiful, or prophetic, according to the distance the soul has separated itself from the body, or to the spiritual society or surroundings in which it may find itself.

In light, instantaneous sleep and awaking, when the soul goes out and in, the dreams will be a confused jumble of illogical sequences, because the soul moves to and fro between sleeping and waking; but in deep sleep, such as young children may have, "whose angels behold the face of God," the soul has entered on its higher life, as apart from that of its prison house, our earthly tabernacle.

Sleep is, then, only a degree of entrancement, and differs from deep entrancement in the soul remaining intact with the body.

Bad dreams may arise from bad health, or from the soul's unwholesome thoughts, or from its associating with those evil spirits which haunt the outside portals of Paradise, and hence the idea of the vampire. But the wholesome and good soul passes rapidly through the door-way and ascends to the society of good spirits; and hence your old men may dream dreams and your young men see visions of that which is prophetic.

Therefore, in composing your soul to sleep, let not the sun go down on your wrath, nor give place to the devil, but calmly commend yourselves to the keeping of our Father who art in Heaven, that His kingdom come.

The myth of Castor and Pollux, each dying daily for the other, may signify this daily sleep and awaking, and if it were possible that we should pass in sleep into Paradise and sup with the angels, we might also participate in their strength, and our years be thus indefinitely prolonged.

Sleep thus got will be "sore labours' bath, balm of hurt minds, chief nourisher in life's feast," and as an aid to those tossing on sleepless beds, many might find, that if they could abstract themselves and fix their spiritual gaze on the deep darkness in which God dwells, and ask for sleep, it might come to them calmly and at once.

BY THE SAME AUTHOR.

Fourth Thousand, Extra Foolscap 8vo, cloth, red edges; price 2/-.

THE LIFE, TEACHINGS, AND WORKS
OF THE
LORD JESUS CHRIST,

Arranged as a continuous Narrative of the Four Gospels, according to the Revised Version.

'This book renders splendid service to all devout students of our Lord's life.'—*Church Times.*

'The most complete account of our Lord's life.'—*Literary Churchman.*

'Much to be commended to the use of Christian Missionaries.'—*The Church Review.*

'In this narrative, so-called discrepancies disappear, and in many ways the gain is striking.'—*The Rock.*

'This book meets a want often felt by Bible Students.'—*Congregationalist.*

'Renders a service which should be gratefully acknowledged. The preface is masterly.'—*Baptist Magazine.*

'Greatly facilitates the study of the Gospels.'—*Nonconformist.*

'A most excellent and useful volume.'—*Evangelical Magazine.*

'We most heartily commend this book.'—*The Freeman.*

'Let the Sunday School Teacher and Bible Student get this book.'—*Illustrated Missionary News.*

'We are not surprised that this book has reached a FOURTH thousand.'—*Congregational Magazine.*

'An efficient aid to the study of the peerless character of Christ.'—*Baptist Magazine.*

'Compiled with signal ability. The preface gives a wonderfully clear and full summary of our Lord's life.'—*New Congregational Magazine.*

'An edifying compendium of the New Testament admirably carried out.'—*Christian Miscellany.*

'The advantages of this book are apparent.'—*Illustrated Missionary News.*

'Executed with admirable discernment, and should be in the hands of every Sunday School Teacher. The preface is a masterly compendium of the life and works of Christ.'—*Methodist S. S. Record.*

'In the deepest and truest sense this is the best life of our Lord extant.'—*Brigham Gazette.*

'An excellent book, and to read it through is to get a wider and broader idea of our Lord's life.'—*Ecclesiastical Chronicle.*

'A most valuable book, the result of very great care and labour.'—*Sunday School Magazine.*

'This beautiful volume renders very valuable service to Students of the Gospel.'—*Methodist Magazine.*

'This book brings a distinctly fresh impression of the majesty and beauty of the Saviour.'—*Sunday School Chronicle.*

'It cannot but be profitable to study the Gospel in the form here presented.'—*The Christian.*

'This is the true life of Christ: it is a work that must last, and should be in the hands of every Bible Student.'—*Methodist Magazine.*

'Invaluable to Bible Students.'—*City Press Magazine.*

'An admirable book.'—*The Literary World.*

'We sincerely thank the Editor for this book.'—*Glasgow Herald.*

'We commend this book very heartily to all Ministers of religion, Sunday School Teachers, and Bible Students.'—*Liverpool Mercury.*

'This book seems to be likely to be very useful to all Students of the Scriptures.'—BISHOP OF GLOUCESTER AND BRISTOL.

'An admirable work.'—JOHN W. SODOR & MAN.

'A valuable book.'—DEAN OF LINCOLN.

'A beautiful and admirable book. There is nothing which so well brings out the life of our Lord. It will, I hope, be in the hands of thousands.'—DEAN OF WINCHESTER.

'I appreciate very much this unique volume.'—REV. W. LEFROY, DEAN OF NORWICH.

'A most useful and interesting book.'—REV. R. W. FORREST, DEAN OF WORCESTER.

'The careful and conscientious preparation of this book I greatly respect and admire.'—REV. JAMES MARTINEAU, D.D.

'The idea of this book is excellent, and merits the widest circulation.'—PROFESSOR BLACKIE.

'We thank the Author most heartily for this book.'—REV. J. KENNEDY, D.D.

'A most useful book.'—THE VICAR OF KENSINGTON.

'This book renders the Church and the world great service.'—THE RECTOR OF CRIEFF.

'An excellent idea, the result of much careful study.'—*Great Thoughts.*

'It is an undoubted gain to have the wonderful story presented in this form.'—REV. W. MOORE, WIMBLEDON.

'I know of no theological writing which in so brief a space contains so profound a view of our Lord's life as is given in the preface.'—J. W. FARQUHAR.

'A most useful book to give to sceptics; many read it with interest as a biography, who will not read the Gospels in their usual form.'—N.B., M.A.

CHISTO-THEOSOPHY PRESS NOTICES.

This is one of the most deeply interesting and valuable works on supersensible science which has appeared for a long time. The author, Dr. George Wyld, formerly President of the British Theosophical Society, is, probably, the profoundest Christian Theosophist of the age. He has for many years been a patient, unselfish, intelligent student of the occult sciences; and the result of his investigations, and his strictly scientific conclusions, as embodied in this work, will be of intense interest to all who believe in something better and higher than sense and matter.—THE PLATONIST (St. Louis).

Dr. Wyld's book contains a series of thoughtful, scholarly, and interesting papers. The moral tone is stimulating and inspiring. Force, learning, and sincerity, are his characteristics. -THE THEOSOPHIST (Bombay).

The whole book is pervaded by the present sense of a noble aim, and no spiritual mind who reads it can fail to obtain from it purer and better views of life.—LIGHT.

The publication of this second edition of Dr. Wyld's book is opportune. In simple English he gives a clear view of the subject. It is a book commendable not only for the high tone that it maintains, but because it presents a manual for the many.—TELEGRAPH.

Dr. George Wyld whose highly intelligent face forms the frontespiece of this book on the all-absorbing subject of Theosophy, is the author of this work which should be accepted as the best book of the movement.-- NEWSAGENT.

Dr. Wyld's portrait prefixed to this book lets us know we have to do with a refined fanatic.—THE FREE THINKER.

This book is interesting from the large collection it contains of authenticated spiritualistic facts. The author is much in earnest.—GLASGOW HERALD.

Chapter XIII. contains a clear sighted comparison of Buddhism and Christianity.—LITERATURE.

Well worth reading—Dr. Wyld is a Christian and Theosophist, and in these characters is consistent.—BOOKSELLER.

Dr. Wyld's work is worth studying as showing how the Christian Church has always recognised the spiritual element in nature and in man.—CHURCH BELLS.

Deeply interesting.—Able, scholarly and reverent, in matter, style and treatment.—Sincerity and conviction mark every line of a book which all students should read.—LYCEUM BANNER.

The idea running through the book is that spirit is the substance of matter, and it traces the highest religion, philosophy, science, poetry and art to the one spiritual centre in the soul of man from which the voice of God speaks.—THE STAR.

A most interesting book. You have sounded the highest key-note of Christian life most clearly and distinctly. Lucidity with depth are your characteristics.—A. I. PENNY.

If your sentiments were commonly appreciated, the world would be flooded with light and beauty.—NEWTON CROSLAND

I am reading your book a second time. I like it exceedingly.—FREDERICK HOCKLEY.

I read your book again and again with great pleasure and entire agreement, and carry it about with me.—REV. MAURICE DAVIES.

I rose from the perusal of your paper on *Man as a Spirit* with intense admiration. It is splendid.—MRS. HALLOCK.

Your views are to me profoundly suggestive.—THE LATE LORD BORTHWICK.

I have read with great interest your papers.—THE HON. RODEN NOEL.

Your book has enraptured me. I have found in it the food I have all my life been lacking.—A. RIDDLE.

Your papers contain thoughtful and beautiful ideas.—REV. MR. MANNERS.

Your union of abstruse science with the deepest spiritual truths is very important. Your mission seems to be to render with clearness mystical obscurities. It is a great gift to be able thus to illuminate.—E. DIETZ.

Your book contains much which interests me, and I agree with you entirely.—A. M. H. WATTS.

You have the faculty of seizing on essentials. Your catena of principals is excellent. Your insights are good and thorough.—REV. A. T. ATWOOD and MRS. ATWOOD.

I experimented, as you describe, with anæsthetics, and obtained an absolute proof of the spiritual world. I saw that spirit was the intensely solid substance of matter, and that external matter was the mere shadow.—R. PALMER THOMAS.

www.ingramcontent.com/pod-product-compliance
Lightning Source LLC
Chambersburg PA
CBHW031943230426
43672CB00010B/2030